G000146895

Literary Strolls around The Cotswolds
and
The Forest of Dean

Gordon Ottewell

Published by Sigma Leisure – an imprint of
Sigma Press, 1 South Oak Lane, Wilmslow, Cheshire SK9 6AR, England.

British Library Cataloguing in Publication Data
A CIP record for this book is available from the British Library.

ISBN: 1-85058-687-X

Maps and photographs: the author
Cover photograph: Willersey *(Gordon Ottewell)*

Typesetting and Design by: Sigma Press, Wilmslow, Cheshire.
Printed by: MFP Design and Print

Disclaimer: the information in this book is given in good faith and is believed to be correct at the time of publication. No responsibility is accepted by either the author or publisher for errors or omissions, or for any loss or injury howsoever caused. Only you can judge your own fitness, competence and experience.

Preface

Every region of England has its literature, inspired by its scenic beauty and distinctive character. Far from being an exception, the Cotswolds must surely rank among the most blessed of these; for centuries, poets and a wide range of other writers, both home-grown and from afar, have recorded their delight in the Cotswold landscape, and in so doing have enriched the region with the beauty of their language and the skill of their expression.

Many of the most memorable examples of the work of these literary figures are associated with specific Cotswold features. These range from lines in praise of particular towns and villages to descriptions of individual views, hilltops, river valleys, or even unusual incidents or other personal experiences.

Without exception, these writers have succeeded in conveying their love of the Cotswold countryside through close and patient observation. They have lingered and looked, savoured and reflected, before moving on. No 'doing' the Cotswolds in a few days for them; as one of their number, the poet W.H. Davies put it

'What is this life if, full of care,
We have no time to stand and stare.'

The aim of this book is to encourage the reader to discover the delights of strolling, standing and staring at some of the Cotswold sights that these men and women have found inspirational. Each of the 40 strolls, none of which exceeds 3 miles in length, has a specific literary connection, which is described in the text. Alternatively, the reader may choose to use the book merely as a stroller's guide, offering as it does a variety of delightful short walks throughout the Cotswolds and beyond.

Whatever one's preference, the strolls should provide hours of healthy enjoyment out-of-doors and on foot in one of the loveliest regions of England.

Gordon Ottewell

Acknowledgements

I wish to record my thanks to the following, all of whom supplied important information used in the compiling of this book:

Philip and Freda Best, Anne and Tony Boden, Janet Bollington and Geoffrey Warren.

Special thanks are due to Bill Cronshaw and his son, William, without whose invaluable assistance this book would have remained merely an idea in the author's mind!

The quotation from John Betjeman's *Summoned by Bells* is reproduced by permission of John Murray, publishers.

Last, but by no means least, my grateful thanks to Margaret, my wife, for her patience and practical help.

Gordon Ottewell.

Contents

Introduction

Using the book   1
Obtaining the recommended books   1

The Walks

Tewkesbury and Winchcombe area

The Countryman Novelist: John Moore at Kemerton   3
Distance: 2 miles

The Footpath Walker: Algernon Gissing at Willersey   6
Distance: 1½ miles

The American who Came to Stay: Mary Anderson at Broadway   10
Distance: 1 mile

The Man behind Peter Pan: J.M. Barrie at Stanway   13
Distance: 2 miles (Short option: 1 mile)

The Windrush Wanderer: Wilson MacArthur at Taddington   17
Distance: 2 miles

The Contented Countrywoman: Margaret Westerling at Ford   20
Distance: 1¾ miles (2½ miles if including Temple Guiting)

Engineer Extraordinary: Tom Rolt at Prescott   23
Distance: 2 miles

Moreton-in-Marsh and Stow-on-the-Wold area

A Farmer's Memories: Aubrey Seymour at Upper Ditchford   28
Distance: 2 miles

Summoned by Bells: John Betjeman at Sezincote   32
Distance: 2¾ miles

The Parson Diarist: Francis Witts at Upper Slaughter   36
Distance: 2¼ miles

Guest at the Rectory: Jane Austen at Adlestrop   40
Distance: 1½ miles

A Broadcaster's Boyhood: Freddy Grisewood at Daylesford   43
Distance: 2¼ miles

The Birdwatching Don: William Warde Fowler at Kingham   46
Distance: 3 miles

Creator of 'The Countryman': J.W. Robertson Scott at Idbury   50
Distance: 2 miles

Cheltenham area

Sketching The Stone: Freda Derrick on Leckhampton Hill   54
Distance: 1½ miles

A War Poet's Brief Peace: Ivor Gurney on Crickley Hill   58
Distance: 1½ miles

The Lady who Lived Alone: Annette Macarthur-Onslow at Pinswell   62
Distance: 2½ miles

The Rural Rider: William Cobbett at Withington   65
Distance: 1¼ miles

Burford and Lechlade area

Hons and Rebels: Nancy and Jessica Mitford at Asthall   69
Distance: 3 miles

Local Girl who Made Good: Mollie Harris at Ducklington   73
Distance: 2 miles

The Jubilee Boy: George Swinford at Filkins   76
Distance: 2½ miles

The Scholar and his Church: John Keble at Southrop   79
Distance: 3 miles

The Poet's Path: Percy Shelley at Lechlade   83
Distance: 1½ miles

The Craftsman's Corner: William Morris at Kelmscott   86
Distance: 2 miles

Cirencester area

The Curious Traveller: H.J. Massingham at Duntisbourne Rouse   90
Distance: 3 miles (short option, three-quarters of a mile)

The Dramatist finds Delight: John Drinkwater at Far Oakridge   93
Distance: 2¼ miles (short option, three-quarters of a mile)

The Roving Craftsman: Norman Jewson at Sapperton   96
Distance: 2¾ miles

The Poet in the Park: Alexander Pope at Cirencester   100
Distance: 3 miles

Squire and Villager: J. Arthur Gibbs at Ablington   103
Distance: 2½ miles

Stroud area

A Cotswold Year: C. Henry Warren at Stockend   107
Distance: 1½ miles

The Cricketing Poet: Frank Mansell at Sheepscombe   111
Distance: 1 mile

A Lifetime in the Valley: Laurie Lee at Slad   114
Distance: 2 miles

The Scholar Poet's Second Home: A.E. Housman at Woodchester   118
Distance: 1 mile

The Tramp-Poet's Last Home: W.H. Davies at Watledge   121
Distance: 1¼ miles

Newent and The Forest of Dean area

A Poet's Patch: W.W. Gibson at Leddington   126
Distance: 2½ miles

Man of Many Parts: John Haines on May Hill   130
Distance: 1¼ miles

The Child in The Forest: Winifred Foley at Brierley   134
Distance: 2¼ miles

A Fool in The Forest: Leonard Clark at Green Bottom   137
Distance: 1¾ miles

The Playwright in his Place: Dennis Potter at Christchurch   140
Distance: 2¾ miles

A Gloucestershire Lad: F.W. Harvey at Minsterworth   143
Distance: 3 miles

Bibliography   147
Tourist Information Centres   148
Index   149

Key to symbols used on sketchmaps

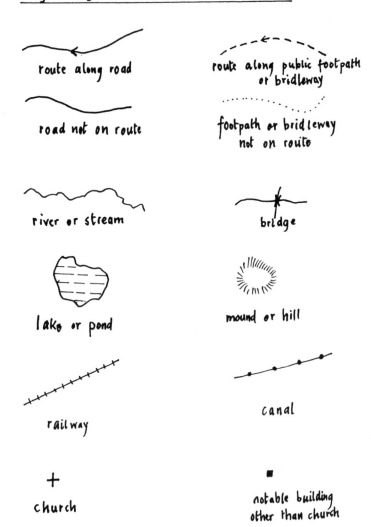

route along road

road not on route

route along public footpath
or bridleway

footpath or bridleway
not on route

river or stream

bridge

lake or pond

mound or hill

railway

canal

church

notable building
other than church

Introduction

Using the book

For convenience, the strolls have been arranged in seven sections:

Tewkesbury and Winchcombe area	7 strolls
Moreton-in-Marsh and Stow-on-the-Wold area	7 strolls
Cheltenham area	4 strolls
Burford and Lechlade area	6 strolls
Cirencester area	5 strolls
Stroud area	5 strolls
Newent and Forest of Dean area	6 strolls

The routes of the strolls are supplemented by notes on parking, the nature of the terrain and suggested hostelries offering refreshment.

A simplified location map appears at the start of each section, showing main towns and roads as well as the precise locations of the individual strolls (underlined). Also provided are detailed sketch maps to accompany each stroll. These are intended not only to complement the route descriptions but also to provide additional information for those wishing to extend the strolls (see *key to symbols*).

Obtaining the recommended books

Many of the books referred to as 'Recommended Reading' in the text are out of print and there is little prospect of them being re-issued, at least not in the immediate future. However, it is well worth enquiring at libraries for copies, as in the writer's experience, librarians will often go to considerable lengths to track down a requested title.

Readers wishing to buy their own copies of out-of-print books are strongly advised to contact their local second-hand bookshop. Many of these establishments offer a booksearch service for titles not currently in stock and, given time, will more often than not obtain books at reasonable prices, allowing for search and postage costs.

The Cotswolds and neighbouring areas covered by this book are especially fortunate in having an excellent range of secondhand and antiquarian bookshops from which to choose. To obtain a current list of these, send a foolscap s.a.e to:

Mrs M.Stephenson, Anchor Bookshop, 88 North Street, Winchcombe, Cheltenham, Gloucestershire GL54 5PS. Tel: 01242-602149

Tewkesbury and Winchcombe area

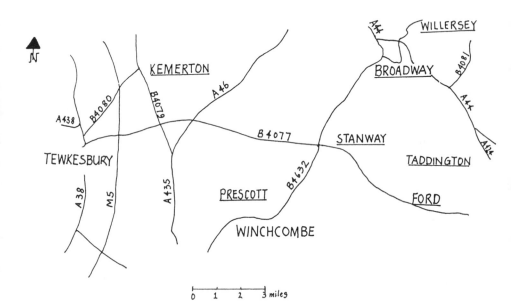

The Countryman Novelist
John Moore at Kemerton

Distance: 2 miles

Location: Kemerton. The village lies between the A435 and the B4080, 5 miles NE of Tewkesbury.

Park and Start: In the village, near the junction of roads by the war memorial (OS Landranger Sheet 150. GR 946372).

Terrain: Along level lanes and footpaths, stretches of which may be muddy after rain. Some of the stiles are primitive.

Refreshments: Crown Inn (near start of stroll).

Route

➤ Walk down the lane which meets the main village street at the war memorial. Keep straight on at a crossroads and continue past the church.

➤ Follow the road as it swings to the right, passing the timber-framed Old Manor and several other attractive thatched cottages.

➤ At a T-junction, turn left along the no-through-road. This is the ap-

Cottage at Kemerton

proach to Lower Mill, for many years the home of John Moore, and where he wrote some of his best-loved books.

➢ In 30 metres, turn right over a stile and keeping a hedge on the left, cross a field to a second stile. Beyond this, continue, still with a hedge on the left, to reach a marker post. Follow the yellow arrow to the left, descending steps to cross a footbridge and reach a wide path. Excellent views now open up, dominated by the wooded Alderton and Dumbleton hills, away to the south east.

➢ Turn left and follow the path towards woodland. On reaching the woodland, turn left once more along a wide field headland, with woodland on the left.

➢ When the path swings sharply to the right, cross a stile on the left alongside a gate and keep a lakeside fence on the left as far as a stile.

➢ Cross this stile and go over a footbridge. In 10 metres, ignore another footbridge on the right. Instead, keep straight on along a wide grassy path with the lake on the left. Continue to pass the remains of an old water mill and on through a gate to reach the road walked earlier.

➢ Turn right back to the start.

Literary Connection

Although the name of John Moore (1907-1967) is associated chiefly with his native Tewkesbury (Elmbury in his famous Brensham Trilogy), he lived for the greater part of his life in the nearby village of Kemerton, on the slopes of Bredon Hill. Boundary changes had resulted in Kemerton being transferred to Worcestershire in 1933, and when the subject of his living outside his native county was raised, Moore made a point of protesting that he could hardly be blamed for the exclusion of his adopted village from Gloucestershire!

As a writer, John Moore's range was wide. His first book, a novel, was published when he was only 23 and was followed by among other early works, a highly readable book on the Cotswolds and a painstakingly researched biography of the poet Edward Thomas. Following a spell as a correspondent covering the Spanish Civil War, he served with distinction as a Fleet Air Arm pilot in the Second World War, after which his Brensham Trilogy secured his place as a widely-read and respected country author.

John Moore's regard for the well being of the natural environment was unswerving. Characteristically he was never afraid to challenge what he regarded as the dangers of technological progress that were making an increasing impact in the countryside. A keen naturalist from

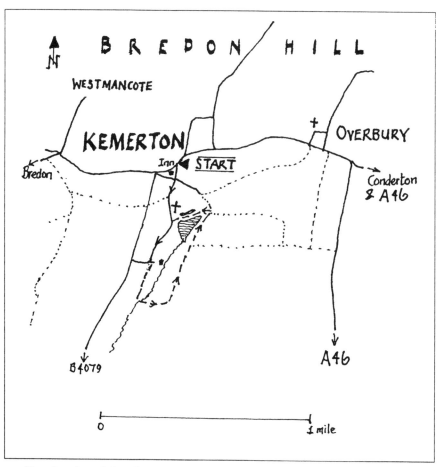

earliest boyhood, he deserves recognition as a pioneer conservationist. It is fitting that a wildlife sanctuary has been established at Kemerton, where he never ceased to find delight in observing the wild inhabitants of his immediate surroundings, and that an excellent countryside museum perpetuates his name in Tewkesbury.

Recommended Reading

The Season of the Year, Come Rain, Come Shine, Man and Bird and Beast and any other of John Moore's numerous books.

Nearby Stroll

Engineer Extraordinary: L.T.C. Rolt at Stanley Pontlarge (p23)

The Footpath Walker

Algernon Gissing at Willersey

Distance: 1½ miles

Location: Willersey. The village lies on the B4632, 1½ miles NE of Broad-way.

Park and Start: On Church Street, a no-through-road opposite the village pond. (O.S. Landranger Sheet 150, GR 106397).

Terrain: Chiefly along field paths, which may be muddy after rain. Gentle gradients.

Refreshments: The Bell Inn and the New Inn (both at Willersey).

Route

➤ Walk along Church Street and enter the churchyard. Take the path to the left of the church and leave the churchyard through a kissing gate to enter a field.

➤ Follow the right-hand yellow waymark, crossing ridge and furrow to go over a stile and a stone-slab bridge.

➤ The path now forks. Keep to the right, ignoring a stile on the left, which will be crossed on the return route. Keep a hedge on the left and continue to cross a stile.

➤ The path now climbs gently to reach a stile in a hedge. Beyond this, follow the left-hand yellow waymark (i.e. straight on) up the left-hand margin of a cherry orchard to cross another stile in the hedge on the left.

➤ The path now crosses a stream and strikes off in zig-zag fashion over more ridge and furrow roughly in the direction of Saintbury church.

➤ Approaching the church, veer slightly to the left to follow a fence and reach a further stile leading to the churchyard gate.

➤ The rugged cross marking William Smith's grave and that of Mary his wife, is visible on the left of the path as it draws level with the church itself.

➤ To return to Willersey, follow the church path down towards the road. Turn left along the pavement and continue as far as a footpath sign indicating a right-of-way along a surfaced lane on the left.

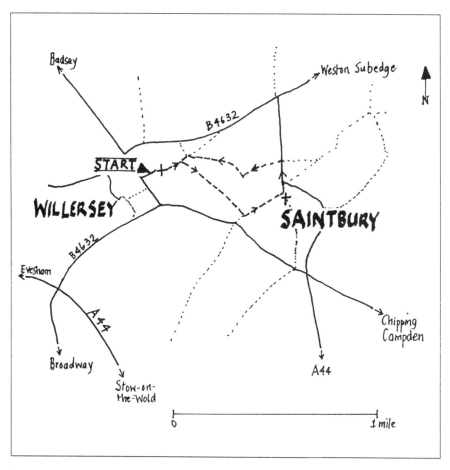

> Pass the telephone box and continue beyond houses to a stile at the lane end.

> Cross a field to reach another. In this second field, follow a fence on the right to cross a stile by a gate. Turn right down a field and cross two stiles.

> In the next field, keep a hedge on the right. On entering another field, go straight over to cross a stile by a large oak tree.

> Turn left, go over two more stiles and rejoin the outward route. Turn right over the stile crossed earlier and retrace your steps back to Willersey church and the start.

Literary Connection

It was on an autumn morning in 1887 that Algernon Gissing, brother of the novelist George, first met the man who was to inspire him to write a delightful book based on his wanderings in the north Cotswolds. Thirty-seven years were to pass before the book *The Footpath-Way in Gloucestershire*, was published, and by that time, William Smith, parish clerk of Saintbury, bass viol player and village road-mender, had been dead for fourteen years.

Gissing, a solicitor by profession, discovered the north Cotswolds on a cycling tour, fell in love with the region and eventually came to live there. His ambition to emulate his famous brother as a novelist ended in failure but his book on Broadway (1904), followed twenty years later by *The Footpath Way in Gloucestershire*, won him well-deserved recognition as a knowledgeable and sensitive recorder of the changing rural scene.

But it is with the association of William Smith, Gissing's friend and inspiration, that this stroll is especially concerned. Born in 1820, the son of a waggoner, Smith received the rudiments of an education from the village rector, who on the death of William's grandfather, Saintbury's parish clerk, installed William in the clerk-

Saintbury church

ship at the tender age of 14. William held this office for 67 years, combining these duties with his work as road-mender, and devoting his leisure hours to music-making both in church and at social events for many miles around. His extensive local knowledge and old-fashioned charm endeared him to Gissing, who's appeal for subscriptions towards a memorial on Smith's death in 1910 resulted in the distinctive gravestone to be seen in Saintbury churchyard.

Gissing's knowledge and love of the north Cotswolds extended to include its rich wildlife and his book contains an eloquent plea for its well-being – an early attempt to promote nature conservation.

Recommended Reading

The Footpath Way In Gloucestershire, Algernon Gissing. Dent. 1924.

Nearby Stroll

The American who came to Stay: Mary Anderson at Broadway (p10).

The American who Came to Stay
Mary Anderson at Broadway

Distance: 1 mile

Location: Broadway. The village stands on the B4632, half a mile south of the A44 and 5 miles SE of Evesham.

Park and Start: The official pay-park off the B4632 Leamington Road. (OS Landranger Sheet 150. GR 110377).

Terrain: Chiefly along pavements but with one short stretch of field walking, which may be muddy after rain. A steady climb up to Court Farm.

Refreshments: Choice of inns and teashops in Broadway.

Route

➤ Leave the car park along the public footpath to the High Street, signposted alongside the toilets. This path emerges in the village close to the junction of High Street and Leamington Road.

➤ Turn left up the eastern end of High Street, which, until the opening of Broadway's long-overdue bypass in 1998, was the A44, carrying a vast amount of through traffic from Evesham towards Oxford and the south via the celebrated Fish Hill. Now, mercifully, this stretch of road provides access to the few houses alongside it only and the stroller can stand and stare without enduring ceaseless noise and noxious fumes as formerly.

➤ Court House (formerly Court Farm, the home of Mary Anderson) is the last house on the right before the old road swings to the right to end in a barrier at the approach to the bypass.

➤ To return partly by public footpath to the car park, follow the signpost to Willersey and Saintbury church below and on the opposite side from Court House (Bibsworth Lane).

➤ At the lane end, instead of turning right under the bypass, cross two stiles on the left to follow a footpath along the edge of a field. Leave over a stile.

➤ The path continues by gardens to reach a road through a kissing gate. Turn right for a short distance to reach another signposted footpath between gardens. This leads to another road.

➤ Turn left along it to reach a T-junction. Turn right here and immediately right again back to the car park.

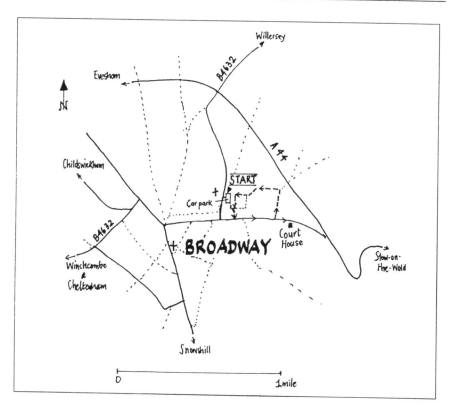

Literary Connection

Broadway, and in particular, the Lygon Arms, became a great attraction for wealthy, cultured people during the early years of the Edwardian era. Among the first to 'discover' the village were the American actress Mary Anderson and her husband Antonio de Navarro, who bought the derelict 17th century Court Farm and later its neighbour, Bell Farm, and converted them into a vast luxury home in which they entertained, amongst others Sir Edward Elgar, A.E Housman, J.M Barrie, Hugh Walpole, Francis Brett Young and a host of other celebrities.

Mary Anderson had relinquished her career as a Shakespearean actress on her marriage but was persuaded to come out of retirement during the First World War to raise money for charity. She also made a spectacular appearance as 'America' at a pageant in the Queen's Hall in London in 1917 on the United States' entry into the war. Noted for her striking good looks, Mary Anderson made a deep and lasting impression on a village boy, Sid Knight, who in his autobiographical *Cotswold*

Broadway

Lad, written half a century later, recalled that after being patted on the head and greeted by 'Madame', as the beautiful incomer was known, he rushed into his cottage to tell his mother 'Mrs God has just spoken to me!'.

It was not until she reached her mid-seventies, and after her husband's death, that Mary Anderson completed her second volume of autobiography, *A Few More Memories* (the first volume, *A Few Memories*, concerning her stage career had been written many years before). A devout Roman Catholic, she was buried in the Catholic burial ground across the Leamington Road from the car park, in which a large flat stone to the left of the chapel door is inscribed

> Mary Anderson
> Born Sacramento 1859
> Died Broadway 1940
> RIP.

Recommended Reading

A Few More Memories. Mary Anderson de Navarro. Hutchinson. 1936
Cotswold Lad. Sid Knight. Phoenix House. 1960.

Nearby Strolls

The Footpath Walker: Algernon Gissing at Saintbury (p6)
The Man behind Peter Pan: J.M. Barrie at Stanway (p13)

The Man behind Peter Pan
J.M. Barrie at Stanway

Distance: 2 miles (Short option: 1 mile)

Location: Stanway, a village off the B4077, 1 mile east of its junction with the B4632 and 4 miles NE of Winchcombe

Park and Start: On the grass verge close to the Cotswold Way footpath sign and opposite the cricket ground at the northern extremity of the village. (OS Landranger sheet 150 GR 061326)

Terrain: Along minor roads and field paths, which may be muddy after rain. Virtually flat throughout.

Refreshments: Old Bakehouse restaurant (on B4077). Mount Inn, Stanton (1½ miles NE). Pheasant Inn and restaurant, Toddington roundabout (1 mile west)

Stanway House and gardens opening times: Tuesday & Thursday 2-5pm, June to September

Route

➤ Opposite the starting point is the thatched cricket pavilion given to the village in 1925 by Sir James Barrie. It replaced a converted railway carriage and stands on staddle stones, formerly used on Cotswold farms as a vermin-proof method of supporting hay ricks.

➤ Walk towards the village. Soon, on the left, is one of the entrances to Stanway House. From the gateway a glimpse can be had of the house itself, as well as its spacious wooded grounds, and away to the right, a magnificent stone-roofed tithe barn, built for the then owner of the manor, the Abbot of Tewkesbury, in 1380.

➤ Continue to reach St. Peter's church. Apart from a fine Jacobean pulpit and a modern altar, the work of the eminent designer Sir Ninian Comper, the interior of the church contains little of interest. However, part of the churchyard wall is worth seeing, as it comprises a stone coffin and other odd fragments of masonry, removed from inside the church by its Victorian restorers. The churchyard also provides a good view of Barrie's beloved Stanway House, and in particular of its immense 60-pane oriel window.

➤ Next to the church stands the elaborate gate house of Stanway House,

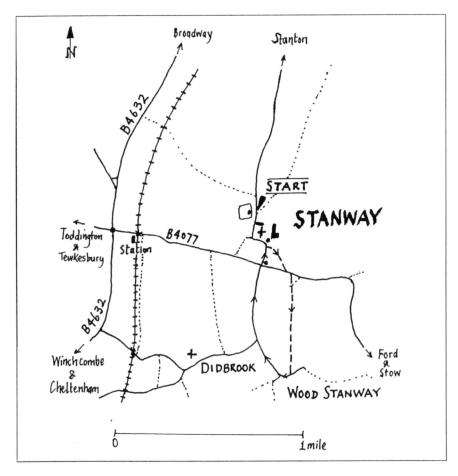

built about 1630 for the Tracy family by the master mason Timothy Strong of Barrington, near Burford, of locally quarried golden-coloured stone. It comprises a mixture of architectural styles and is richly decorated with scallop shell ornamentation, in keeping with the emblem of the Tracy family.

➤ Beyond the high wall, follow the Cotswold Way footpath to the left and through a kissing gate (noting the swan's head carving) to cross an old orchard and reach the B4077.

➤ To complete the short stroll, turn right along the pavement and right again at the crossroads (noting the striking war memorial) to reach and retrace the outward route.

> To continue the longer stroll, turn left along the pavement and in a short distance, cross to continue along the Cotswold Way by a field path to the hamlet of Wood Stanway.

> To return to Stanway, follow the road to the right. Keep to the right at a fork and continue to a second fork. Again keep to the right to reach the B4632.

> Cross with care, noting the bronze St. George and dragon war memorial, the work of Alexander Fisher with lettering by Eric Gill. Continue down into Stanway and retrace the outward route back to the start.

Stanway gatehouse

Literary Connection

Between 1923 and 1932, J.M. (later Sir James) Barrie spent several weeks of the summer at Stanway House, renting the building from the Earl of Wemyss, an arrangement made possible through his friendship with Lady Cynthia Asquith, the Earl's daughter.

Barrie had first visited Stanway in 1921 and had immediately been captivated by its old-world charm. Always a keen cricketer he managed to get the Australian cricket team, who were playing at Cheltenham, to take part in a match against a local 11. Later, he founded his own team, comprising literary friends and known as the Allahakbarries, and over the years the villagers became used to encountering such celebrities as A P Herbert, H.G. Wells, A.E.W. Mason, Harley Granville-Barker and Sir Arthur Conan Doyle on their cricketing and literary visits.

One of the most memorable matches played by the Allahakbarries was at Broadway against a team of artists and singers recruited by the American actress Mary Anderson, a resident there (see p10). Recalling her friend's cricketing prowess – or lack of it – in later years, Mary Anderson wrote: *The brilliant Barrie was not a shining light on the cricket field. I never saw him make a single run.* He seems to have faired better as a bowler, however, and it is said that his gift of a new pavilion to the village was prompted by his achieving of a hat-trick in one of the games.

There is an often repeated legend that Barrie got the idea for the fairy Tinkerbell in *Peter Pan* from waking one morning to see the dancing image of a golden cockerel reflected on his bedroom wall from its lofty perch on St. Peter's church. However, as *Peter Pan* was written several years before its author's first recorded visits to Stanway, this seems highly unlikely, to say the least!

Recommended Reading

Peter Pan. J.M. Barrie. 1904

Nearby Strolls

The Contented Countrywoman: Margaret Westerling at Ford (p20)

The Windrush Wanderer: Wilson MacArthur at Taddington (p17)

The Windrush Wanderer
Wilson MacArthur at Taddington

Distance: 2 miles

Location: Taddington, a hamlet on the unclassified road between Snowshill and the B4077 (Stow-on-the-Wold – Tewkesbury road) at Ford.

Park and Start: By a wall opposite cottages at the southern end of the hamlet, near a public footpath sign (OS Landranger Sheet 150. GR 087311).

Terrain: Chiefly along tracks and fieldpaths, which may be muddy after rain. Flat apart from one short climb.

Refreshments: The Plough Inn, Ford (on the B4077, 1 mile south of Cutsdean).

Route

➤ Follow the public footpath sign over a stile and down a field to a second stile. The footpath now follows the infant Windrush along its gently curving valley.

➤ Cross a footbridge (a stone slab when MacArthur came this way) and bear to the right to pass through a handgate. The path now winds up the gently-sloping valley side to pass through another handgate and reach a fork.

➤ Go to the right through a field gate in the direction of a large barn. Pass through two more gates to reach Cutsdean.

➤ Turn right. On the right, a short way down the slope, can be seen the village sheepwash, abandoned and overgrown in MacArthur's time but now happily restored.

➤ At the foot of the slope, turn left. The plain little church of St James, standing in a farmyard containing interesting barns, is on the right.

➤ Continue through the village. Immediately beyond the 'Cutsdean' sign, turn left along a track. This ends at a bend but the route continues as a footpath, with a boundary on the left.

➤ Taddington soon comes into view on the left, with the humps and hollows of the lost medieval village, which escaped MacArthur's attention, visible to the right of the present buildings.

➤ As the footpath nears the hedged lane to Taddington, it crosses a field to reach the lane over a stile. Turn left to cross the well-named Dirty

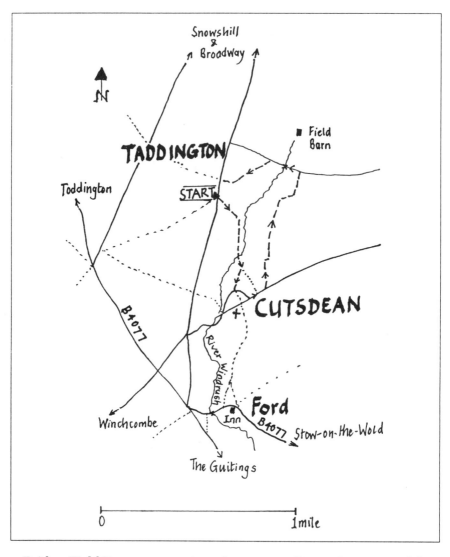

Bridge. Field Barn, now a private house, standing at the source of the Windrush, can be seen to the right.

➤ On reaching a stile on the left by a power pole, those wishing to return to the start by the footpath skirting the site of the lost village should cross and follow the waymark over three stiles. Otherwise, keep straight on to reach a road and turn left along it into Taddington.

Literary Connection

The travel writer Wilson MacArthur, accompanied by his wife Joan, walked the lengths of several English rivers during the later 1940s. His book, *The River Windrush*, first published in December 1946, is a highly readable and well-illustrated account of their adventures.

The MacArthurs began their journey to find the source of the Windrush one sunny day in September. They arrived at Moreton-in-Marsh by train from Paddington and after studying their map, set off to walk towards Taddington, carrying their tent and provisions with them. After camping overnight in the field of a friendly farmer near Bourton-on-the-Hill, the explorers pressed on to reach the lane to Taddington along which, at Dirty Bridge, they at last discovered the object of their search, the source of the Windrush.

Soon, they were following the tiny rivulet down the valley to Cutsdean, where helpful children directed them to the village shop – "a wooden shack, with a corrugated zinc roof beside a little old cottage, trim and neat" – from which they bought potato crisps, lemonade and writing paper with matching envelopes – all for tenpence.

Leaving Cutsdean, MacArthur reflected on the friendliness of the Cotswold people: "We could not help feeling that the Windrush itself had some hand in this friendly spirit, for it is everywhere a pleasant, friendly, open-hearted stream."

The source of The Windrush

Recommended Reading

The River Windrush, Wilson MacArthur. Cassell. 1946.

Nearby Strolls

The Contented Countrywoman: Margaret Westerling at Ford (p20).
The Man behind Peter Pan: J.M. Barrie at Stanway (p13).

The Contented Countrywoman
Margaret Westerling at Ford

Distance: 1¾ miles (2½ miles if including Temple Guiting)

Location: Ford, a hamlet on the B4077, 4 miles east of Winchcombe.

Park and Start: As near as possible to the Plough Inn (patrons may use the Inn car park). (OS Landranger Sheet 163. GR 088295).

Terrain: A mixture of roadside verge, minor road and footpaths, with two short climbs.

Refreshments: The Plough Inn, Ford.

Route

> From the Inn, follow the B4077 down through the hamlet, crossing the bridge over the infant River Windrush before turning off to the left to follow a bridleway climbing out of the valley.

> On reaching a road, turn left along it and follow it for almost

Notice on the Plough Inn at Ford

half a mile, passing Hyde Farm on the right and continuing almost as far as a Temple Guiting sign. Within 20 metres of this, watch for a stone public footpath marker on the left.

> Go through a gate and down a field, passing to the right of a clump of trees to reach a stile in a fence. Beyond, continue the descent, keeping to the right in the next field to cross the Windrush once more over a footbridge.

> Climb slightly to the right up the bank and cross a narrow field to

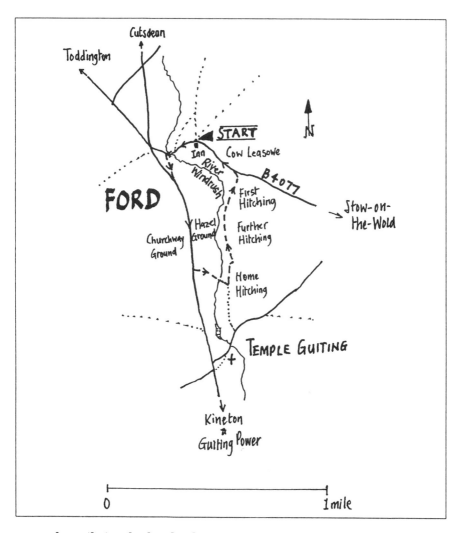

reach a stile in a hedge, leading to a wide track. The village of Temple Guiting lies barely a quarter of a mile distant to the right.

➤ To complete the stroll, turn left. Immediately after a right-hand bend, leave the track to follow another, branching off to the left.

➤ Continue along this as far as a stile in a hedge on the left. From this point it is but a short distance to the B4077.

➤ Turn left along the verge back to Ford and the start.

Literary Connection

Praising Margaret Westerling's book, *Country Contentments* on its publication in 1939, a reviewer wrote: 'it is a record of clear perception and deep appreciations, a happily named testimony of satisfaction in a life spent among the old solid country harmonies in a region quintessentially English'.

To the modern reader, *Country Contentments* is more than that. It is also an invaluable record of day-to-day country life – farming, craftsmanship, customs and traditions – made in the nick of time before the Second World War obliterated the old way of life for ever and presented without a trace of the cloying sentimentality that mars so many books of this kind. Margaret Westerling lived at Ford, knew the little place and its inhabitants intimately, and rejoiced in exploring every facet of its history. Her book was written in the form of a monthly diary and although her travels took her further afield in Gloucestershire and beyond, it is to her own corner of the North Cotswolds that she always returns, eager to share some new discovery, be it archaeological remains, a rare wild flower, a craft technique as described by an elderly practitioner, or a humorous anecdote recorded in the authentic local dialect.

Like all true lovers of the countryside, Margaret Westerling made virtually all her journeys of discovery on foot, following footpaths and bridleways wherever possible, and in so doing observing details of the rural scene all too often overlooked by the hurrying tourist. One of her interest was field names and *Country Contentments* contains a map showing these in the neighbourhood of Ford, some of which are reproduced on the sketch map accompanying this stroll.

Recommended Reading

Country Contentments Margaret Westerling. Constable. 1939.

Nearby Strolls

The Windrush Wanderer: Wilson MacArthur at Taddington (p17).

The Man Behind Peter Pan:. J.M. Barrie at Stanway (p13).

Engineer Extraordinary
Tom Rolt at Prescott

Distance: 2 miles

Location: The hamlet of Prescott lies off the unclassified Gretton –
Gotherington road, 2½ miles west of Winchcombe.

Park and Start: Although the stroll itself commences from the junction of the
no-through-road signposted Prescott, close to the entrance to the Hill Climb,
parking is very difficult here. Instead, it is suggested that cars are parked on
the verge between the Dixton turn and the railway bridge, a quarter of a mile
in the direction of Gotherington. (OS Landranger Sheet 163. GR 300986).

Terrain: Chiefly along bridleways (surfaced and unsurfaced). Steepish
climbs from start, followed by gentle descents.

Refreshments: The Bugatti Inn and the Royal Oak Inn, Gretton. The Shutter
Inn, Gotherington.

Route

➤ From the junction of the Gretton – Gotherington road with the
Prescott signpost, follow this no-through-road as far as a bridleway
sign on the right just before a house.

➤ Stony and rough at first, the bridleway is eventually surfaced and
climbs between trees with the Hill Climb on the right. Although on
event days, cars completing the hill climb return along this lane, they
travel slowly and present no danger to walkers.

➤ At the entrance to Prescott House, the bridleway swings to the left
and reverts once more to its roughly-surfaced state. Continue along
it, still climbing, for almost a quarter of a mile, to reach a junction
with another bridleway at a point where the slope levels out (no
waymark).

➤ Turn sharp right to follow this bridleway through a gate, with a fence
on the right at first. The climb now offers rich scenic rewards on a
clear day, with the main Cotswold escarpment dominant away to the
far right, Bredon Hill and its associated outliers on the right, Dixton
Hill straight ahead and the Malverns also ahead in the far distance.

➤ The descending bridleway skirts the wooded grounds of Prescott
House before winding past a rambling old farm house and finally de-

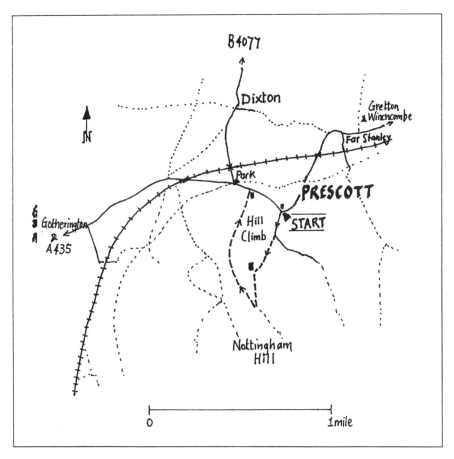

scending, with the Hill Climb again to the right, to reach the Gretton – Gotherington road roughly midway between the Prescott turn and the suggested parking place at the turning to Dixton.

Literary Connection

Since its creation in 1938, the Prescott Hill Climb has long been a mecca for lovers of vintage racing cars. The sight of these splendid vehicles, and of other well-loved and maintained cars of yesteryear, is a familiar one around Prescott on event weekends, while the presence of an inn named after the celebrated Bugatti at nearby Gretton is a further reminder of the Hill Climb's impact on the local scene.

However, Prescott Hill Climb is but one of many achievements of the

Walkers and racing car on Prescott Hill

multi-talented engineer and author Lionel Thomas Caswall Rolt, (1910-1974), always known as Tom, whose home was nearby at the hamlet of Stanley Pontlarge.

Born in Chester, Tom moved with his parents first to Hay-on-Wye before a final move to Gloucestershire in 1920. After six unhappy years at boarding school, he persuaded his father to allow him to leave and to begin an engineering apprenticeship, working on steam engines and later, on the development of a diesel lorry.

Work with high-quality cars followed and Tom became a founder member of the Vintage Sports Car Club. But by 1938 his interest had turned to canals and with his wife he set out to explore the country's inland waterways in a traditional narrow boat, the 'Cressy'. One result of these adventures was a best-selling book, *Narrow Boat*, which brought him national recognition and led to the formation of the Inland Waterways Association.

By 1951 however, Tom Rolt's boundless energies were directed to railways, and in particular to the Talyllyn, a narrow-gauge line in mid-Wales, then threatened with closure. His efforts not only saved the line but led to him becoming a leading figure in the field of industrial history and the last twenty years of his life saw him emerge as a prolific author on a wide range of industrial topics, including biographies of Brunel, Telford and the Stephensons.

His autobiographical trilogy reveals yet another aspect of this remarkable man – a deep and abiding love of the English countryside.

Recommended Reading

Landscape With Machines. Sutton.

Landscape With Canals. Sutton

Landscape With Figures. Sutton.

All written by L.T.C. Rolt.

Nearby Strolls

The Countryman Novelist: John Moore at Kemerton (p3).

The Man Behind Peter Pan: J.M. Barrie at Stanway (p13).

Moreton-in-Marsh and Stow-on-the-Wold area

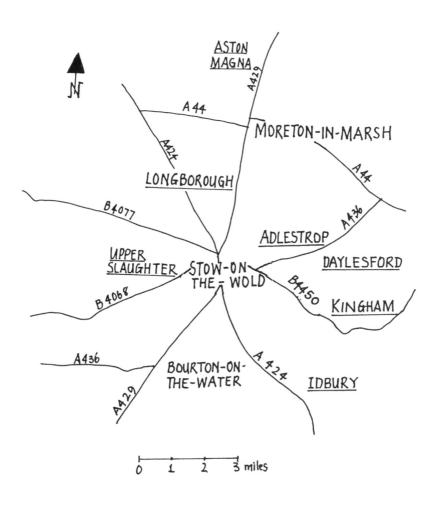

A Farmer's Memories
Aubrey Seymour at Upper Ditchford

Distance: 2 miles

Location: Upper Ditchford lies half a mile north of Aston Magna and 1½ miles west of the A429.

Park and Start: Aston Magna. The village lies off the A429, 2½ miles north of Moreton-in-Marsh. Park as near as possible to the railway bridge, from which the stroll begins. (OS Landranger Sheet 151. GR 199358).

Terrain: Along minor roads and footpaths, which may be muddy after rain. Gentle gradients only.

Refreshments: A choice of inns at Moreton-in-Marsh or village pubs at Blockley, Stretton-on-Fosse, and Paxford.

Route

➤ From the lower end of the railway bridge, follow the public footpath sign to the left. The path soon swings to the right and descends, with gardens on the right.

➤ On reaching a road, turn left along it for a short distance, to reach another footpath sign on the right. Follow this path, with a hedge on the left, to cross the Knee Brook over a footbridge.

➤ Neighbrook, for many years the home of the farming author Aubrey Seymour, stands on the higher ground straight ahead. According to Seymour, it dates from the 17th century.

➤ Follow the waymark across the field diagonally left to reach the Neighbrook drive through a handgate. Turn left. The humpy field on the right is the site of the abandoned village of Upper Ditchford, one of three Ditchford villages which all met a similar fate.

➤ Pass a footpath sign on the right and continue along the drive as far as a bridge at a left-hand bend. Leave the drive here to follow a public footpath on the right. Go through a handgate and keep a hedge on the left. At its end, cross a ditch and go over a field to reach a road over a stile.

➤ Turn left and follow this minor road for about half a mile, passing one public footpath sign on the right and continuing to reach a second.

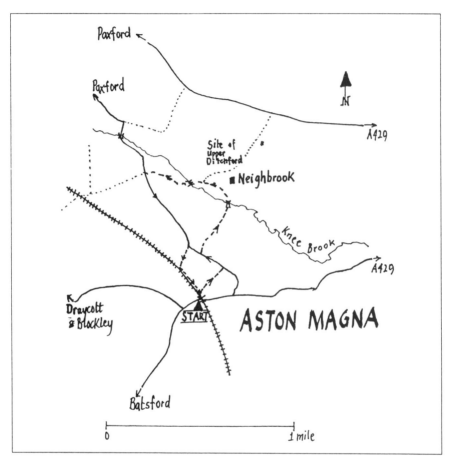

> This path climbs to reach another path on the left, alongside the railway. Follow it back to the bridge from which the stroll commenced.

Literary Connection

In 1968, an 80-year-old retired farmer published his first book, compiled largely from articles written for newspapers and magazines, in which he related in an engaging style somewhat reminiscent of such country writers as A.G. Street and Adrian Bell, his memories of a lifetime spent farming in and around the North Cotswolds.

The Land Where I Belong proved so popular that Aubrey Seymour's publisher brought out a second impression a few months later. Two more volumes followed: *Fragrant the Fertile Earth* and *A Square Mile of*

Cottages, Aston Magna

Old England, the latter appearing shortly after the author's death in the spring of 1972.

In a farming life extending over 60 years, Aubrey Seymour witnessed profound changes in the Cotswold countryside. He saw the demise of the working horse and its replacement by the tractor. He watched as the era of mixed farming was superseded by the specialisation that has become the norm today. He observed the virtual disappearance of a host of colourful country characters – tradesmen, itinerant labourers, fellow farmers – whose presence enlivened and enriched his early years working a remote Cotswold farm.

This is not to say that Aubrey Seymour's books are merely a sentimental longing for the past; on the contrary, a cheerful acceptance of change, spiced with plenty of humorous anecdotes, livens his text, as the concluding sentence of *The Land Where I Belong* testifies: 'I have had a wonderful life, and if I were given the chance to start afresh as a boy, I would choose to be a farmer again'.

Aubrey Seymour was more than just a farmer however. A devotee of Gilbert White's *Natural History of Selborne* from boyhood, he was a knowledgeable field naturalist, a keen and accomplished angler and a good shot. Living for over twenty years at Upper Ditchford, between

Chipping Campden and Moreton-in-Marsh, he was able to get to know every facet of the local countryside and found in it the interest and delight that only the true countryman can discover.

Recommended Reading

The Land Where I Belong. 1968

Fragrant the Fertile Earth. 1970

A Square Mile of Old England. 1972

All by Aubrey Seymour. Published by Roundwood Press, Kineton, Warwickshire.

Nearby Stroll

Summoned By Bells: John Betjeman at Sezincote (p32).

Summoned by Bells

John Betjeman at Sezincote

Distance: 2¾ miles

Location: Longborough. The village stands at the junction of three unclassified roads, midway between the A424 and the A429, 2½ miles north of Stow-on-the-Wold.

Park and Start: In the vicinity of the war memorial situated on a tiny green opposite the Coach and Horses Inn. (OS Landranger Sheets 163 and 151. GR 179297).

Terrain: Chiefly along clearly-defined footpaths, though with one short stretch along a quiet unclassified road. One fairly steep stretch along an estate road.

Refreshments: Coach and Horses Inn, Longborough.

Sezincote House and Gardens: Open Thurs & Fri afternoons, May-Sept.

Route

➤ From the war memorial, and with the Coach and Horses inn on the left, climb the short distance to reach a public footpath sign, indicating Sezincote and Bourton-on-the-Hill, on the right.

➤ A surfaced driveway to begin with, the route soon becomes a footpath, passing along the edge of allotments before entering a field through a handgate. Continue along the clear path (part of the Heart of England Way) for about three-quarters of a mile to reach a surfaced estate road descending from the Longborough to Bourton-on-the-Hill road to a large house.

➤ Continue straight on with fenced woodland on the left. In a short distance, the path veers slightly to the right (watch for a waymark on section of felled tree-trunk) and descends the field towards a gateway. Sezincote House soon comes into view, with its highly distinctive Mogul appearance, of which its onion-shaped copper dome cannot fail to catch the eye.

➤ The footpath continues through Sezincote Park and on to Bourton-on-the-Hill. However, as the purpose of the stroll is to view the House, and as this disappears from view beyond the belt of wood-

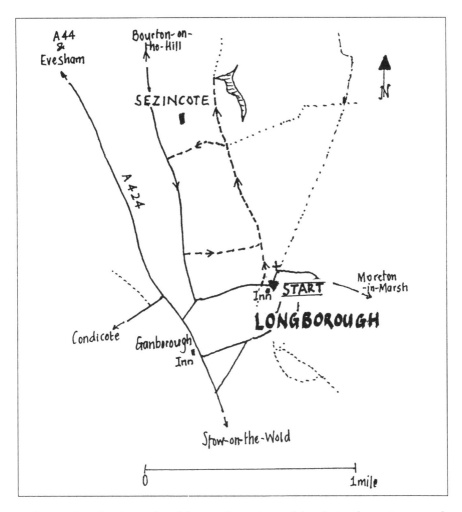

land ahead, steps should now be retraced back to the estate road crossed earlier.

➤ Turn right up this road to reach the Longborough-Bourton road. This road commands extensive views eastwards over the Evenlode valley into Oxfordshire, with Stow-on-the-Wold church dominant away to the south. Turn left now and continue for rather less than half a mile, as far as a public footpath on the left. This keeps a hedge on the left down to the path walked earlier. Turn right along this path back to the start.

Sezincote House

Literary Connection

Once a remote village, Sezincote has since the early 19th century con-
sisted of an Indian-style mansion, designed by the architect Samuel
Pepys Cockerell for his brother Charles, on his return from service in
the East India Company. This amazing house, said to have been the
model on which the Brighton Pavilion was based, was bought by the
Dugdale family in the 1880s and it was here that John Betjeman stayed
while a student at Oxford in the 1920s.

Sezincote, and in particular the Dugdales, made a profound impression on the aspiring poet. He was especially drawn to Ethel Dugdale,
mother of his university friend John, and years later dedicated his first
book of poems, *Mount Zion*, to her, at the same time declaring that the
happiest days of his life had been spent at Sezincote.

It followed that the house and its inhabitants should figure prominently in Betjeman's autobiographical poem *Summoned by Bells*, published in 1960. In a much-quoted passage of this work, the poet recalls
his delight at hearing the distant church bells from the
'wood-smoke-scented luxury' of his weekend retreat:

> *'At six o'clock from Bourton-on-the-Hill,*
> *The bells rang out above the clumps of oak;*
> *A lighter peal from Longborough lingered on;*
> *Moreton-in-Marsh came echoing from the vale.'*

The Dugdale gravestones, overgrown yet still decipherable, can be found in their family enclosure in Longborough churchyard, to the west of the church. They include that of F.B. Dugdale, who won the VC in the Boer War, only to die in a hunting accident at the age of 25.

Recommended Reading

Summoned by Bells (verse autobiography) John Murray 1960.

Young Betjeman. Bevis Hillier. John Murray. 1988.

Nearby Stroll

A Farmer's Memories: Aubrey Seymour at Ditchford (p28)

The Parson Diarist

Francis Witts at Upper Slaughter

Distance: 2¼ miles

Location: Upper Slaughter. The village lies between the A436 and the B4068, 3 miles SW of Stow-on-the-Wold.

Park and Start: The small parking area near the church (OS Landranger Sheet 163. GR 156232).

Terrain: Chiefly along well used footpaths with short stretches of minor road walking. One gentle gradient near start. Muddy patches after rain.

Refreshments: Restaurants only at the Slaughters. Wide choice of inns and cafes at Bourton-on-the-Water.

Route

➤ From the car park, walk along the road indicated as being unsuitable for motors. Pass the former school and descend to the right to cross the tiny River Eye by a footbridge.

➤ Turn right along the lane to reach a road. Turn right again, cross the Eye once more, and continue as far as a public footpath sign on the left. The path leads to yet another bridge over the Eye, beyond which is the first of many kissing gates encountered on the stroll.

➤ Instead of taking the well-worn path up the slope ahead (return route) climb to the left. This less obvious path passes by a gate on the left, leading to a road and continues to reach another gate leading to a second field (yellow waymark on post).

➤ In this field, keep a hedge on the right at first. When this veers away to the right, maintain the original course over the field to reach a gate. Beyond this, the path converges with the road on the left, eventually reaching it over a stile.

➤ Turn right. In about 170 metres, leave the road over a stile on the right and follow the public footpath sign over another stile and across a large horse paddock to reach a road via two kissing gates in a belt of woodland.

➤ Turn right into Lower Slaughter. To see the village, ignore the foot-path sign on the right at a sharp left-hand bend. Instead, continue straight on, eventually passing the church on the left, behind which

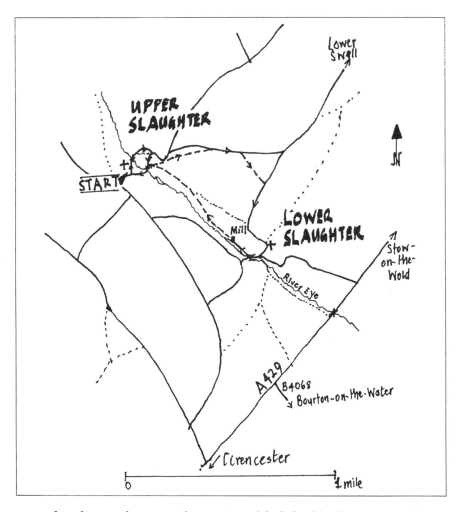

can be glimpsed a magnificent six-gabled double dovecote, said to
date from the 16th Century.

➤ On reaching a road fork, turn right and keep right along the access
road into the village. At its end, follow the causeway by the Eye to
reach the former corn mill (now a museum).

➤ Immediately beyond the mill, turn left along a public footpath (signposted Wardens' Way). This path, gravelled at first, passes through
two kissing gates and keeps to the riverside for about quarter of a
mile. Beyond a third kissing gate, it continues as a field path over old

ridge and furrow, passing through two more kissing gates before descending a slope (view of Rev. Witts's former rectory – now Lords of
Manor Hotel – on left) to reach the footbridge crossed on the outward
route.
➤ Retrace steps to the road and turn left to see the rest of Upper Slaughter, passing the entrance to the Lords of the Manor Hotel before reaching the car park.

Literary Connection

The publication in 1978 of extracts from the diaries of the Rev. Francis
Edward Witts (1783-1854) brought to light a remarkable record of life in
the north Cotswolds during the first half of the 19th century. The 90
notebooks from which
*The Diary of a Cotswold
Parson* was compiled
contained the day-to-
-day jottings of a man
who combined his role
as rector of Upper
Slaughter with that of
magistrate, chairman of
the local board of guard-
ians and trustee of a
provident bank. Witts
also led an active social
life, which took him, by
carriage and on horse-
back, over much of
Gloucestershire and be-
yond when turnpike
roads were a recent fea-
ture and railways in
their infancy.

Francis Witts suc-
ceeded his uncle as rec-
tor of Upper Slaughter
in 1808, the year in
which he married. His
wealth was such that in
1852, two years before

Upper Slaughter church

his death, he was able to buy the lordship of the manor of Upper Slaughter. The then rectory, dating from the 17th century, is now the Lords of the Manor Hotel.

Such was the esteem in which Witts was held that on his death, a sumptuous mortuary chapel was constructed north of the chancel in St. Peter's church.

Recommended Reading

The Diary of a Cotswold Parson. Edited by David Verey. Sutton. 1978-81.

Nearby Strolls

Summoned by Bells: John Betjeman at Sezincote (p32).

Guest at the Rectory
Jane Austen at Adlestrop

Distance: 1½ miles

Location: Adlestrop. The village lies off the A436, 3 miles east of Stow-on-the-Wold.

Park and Start: The village hall car park (OS Landranger Sheet 163. GR242272)

Terrain: Quiet roads and footpaths, which may be muddy after rain. Virtually level throughout.

Refreshments: The Fox Inn, Lower Oddington. (1½ miles SW).

Route

➤ From the car park, turn left. The road forks immediately. One of the name boards from the railway station, closed in the 1960s, stands in a shelter at the junction, with the poem by Edward Thomas, which immortalised the village, on a plate fixed to a platform seat.

➤ Take the right fork. The road climbs gently to another junction. Turn right along the no-through-road leading to the church, which contains early 19th century memorial tablets and windows to members of the Leigh family, to whom Jane Austen was related.

➤ Opposite the church stands Adlestrop House, formerly the rectory at which Jane stayed with her uncle, Revd. Thomas Leigh, on at least three occasions.

➤ The stroll continues down a lane alongside the churchyard. At its foot, go through a kissing gate and follow the perimeter of a cricket field to join a track leading towards a lodge on the A436. A good view of Adlestrop Park can be had behind on the left.

➤ On reaching a clump of oaks to the right of the track, turn off along an indistinct sunken path, keeping the trees on the right. This path crosses the park to reach a road over two stiles.

➤ Turn right to pass a lake. The site of the former railway station, on the Paddington – Hereford line, is on the left, with the River Evenlode alongside.

➤ Beyond the lake, watch for a public footpath sign on the right. Cross

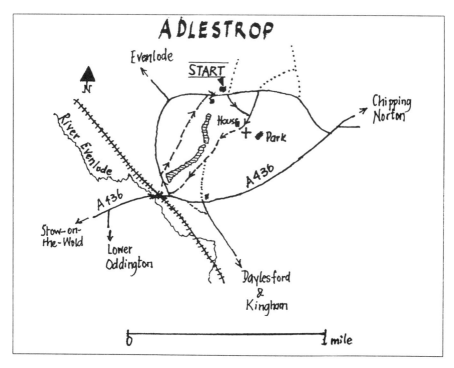

the stile and follow the path, which skirts a field before crossing a footbridge and a field to reach a road over a stile.

➤ Turn right back to the village hall car park.

Literary Connection

Although it is through Edward Thomas's much-loved poem *Adlestrop* that this village in the Evenlode valley is best known, the poet's acquaintance was confined to a brief impression gained when his express train stopped at its little station 'unwontedly' one afternoon in June 1914.

Over a century earlier, however, Adlestrop earned its place on the literary map on account of several visits paid by the novelist Jane Austen, who with her mother stayed at the rectory (now Adlestrop House), the home of her uncle, the Revd Thomas Leigh. Leighs had owned Adlestrop Park since the 16th century and at the time of the nineteen-year-old Jane's first visit, in 1794, her mother's second cousin, James Henry Leigh, was squire.

By 1806, Jane's last recorded visit to the rectory, sweeping changes

Adlestrop House, formerly the rectory

had taken place at Adlestrop. James Henry Leigh had called in the prominent landscape designer Humphry Repton to re-model the village and to lay out extensive gardens in the enlarged park. The proud owner is said to have taken his novelist cousin on a tour of his improved estate and this, according to students of Austen's works, suggests that Mansfield Park, in the novel of that name written in 1811, is based on Adlestrop Park as Jane saw it a few years earlier.

It was during this visit too that the Revd Thomas Leigh received word that he was in line to inherit Stoneleigh Abbey, Warwickshire, following the death of the Hon. Mary Leigh. As immediate occupancy was deemed necessary, the rector, accompanied by Jane and her mother, set off to take possession, and the description of Sotherton Court in *Mansfield Park*, tallies so closely with Stoneleigh, experts believe that it provides conclusive proof that the novel stemmed from Jane's experiences during that eventful summer of 1806.

Recommended Reading

Mansfield Park. Jane Austen (first published 1814).

Nearby Strolls

A Broadcaster's Boyhood: Freddy Grisewood at Daylesford (p43).
The Birdwatching Don: William Warde Fowler at Kingham (p46).

A Broadcaster's Boyhood
Freddy Grisewood at Daylesford

Distance: 2¼ miles

Location: Daylesford. The village lies half a mile off the A436, 4 miles east of Stow-on-the-Wold.

Park and Start: By the church. (OS Landranger Sheet 163. GR 243259).

Terrain: Partly along roadside verges but chiefly along tracks and footpaths, which may be muddy after rain. Virtually level throughout.

Refreshments: The Fox Inn, Lower Oddington. The Plough Inn, Kingham. The Mill Hotel, Kingham.

Route

➢ From the church, walk along the road leading towards the A436. In a quarter of a mile, follow a public footpath sign through a gate on the left. Cross a field diagonally to reach the A436 via a handgate.

➢ Cross and turn left along the pavement of this busy road. Go over the railway bridge and continue as far as the minor road on the left signposted Lower Oddington.

➢ Follow this road into the village. Beyond the Fox Inn, the road bends to the right. Continue as far as a lane on the left, signposted to St Nicholas's church.

➢ This church, reached in about one third of a mile, stands on the site of the original village of Oddington. It fell into disuse in

Warren Hastings memorial,
Daylesford church

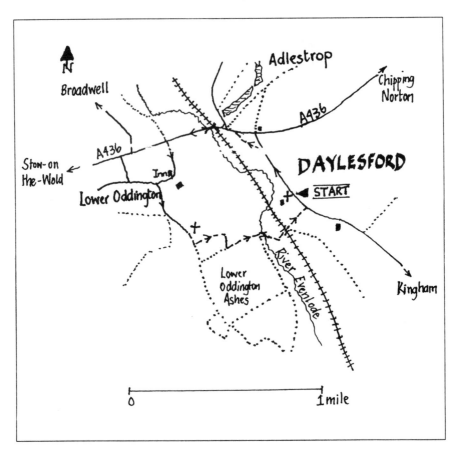

the 19th century and its magnificent wall paintings, long hidden beneath whitewash, were forgotten. Since 1912, however, the church
has been brought back into use and its paintings painstakingly restored.

➤ Beyond the church, turn left to follow a signposted public footpath
along a field edge. On reaching a ditch at a field corner, turn right
alongside it and continue as far as a hedge gap on the left.

➤ Follow the bridleway (blue arrow), with a hedge on the right, as far as
a gap between two fine oaks. Cross a field corner to a footbridge spanning the River Evenlode.

➤ Go over another field to a gate, beyond which a track climbs gently to
cross a railway bridge.

➢ Keep a hedge on the left. (The rectory where Freddy Grisewood spent his boyhood is clearly visible away to the left). On reaching a road, turn left back to the church.

Literary Connection

This tiny village, on the Gloucestershire side of the border with Oxfordshire, was the birthplace of Frederick (Freddy) Grisewood, (1888-1972), the popular broadcaster and former chairman of 'Any Questions?' and 'Gardeners' Question Time'. Born the son of the rector, Grisewood spent an idyllic boyhood in the fields and woods by the local river, the Evenlode, building boats, fishing for trout and crayfish, and developing ball-game skills that were later to win him considerable success at cricket and lawn tennis.

After University and war service, Grisewood returned to Daylesford as agent to Charles Baring Young at Daylesford Park Estate. Living by now at the neighbouring village of Kingham, he got the idea of collecting humorous stories in the Cotswold dialect as told to him by a villager and after successfully trying these out on the BBC, which he had joined in 1929, he published them as *Our Bill* some years later, when they were so well received that the book went to six editions.

On his retirement from full-time broadcasting, Grisewood published a highly-readable account of his varied life (*The World Goes By.* 1952). And although he spent his later years in Hampshire, a commemorative stone in his memory can be seen on his father's grave in the churchyard, not far from the neo-Greek monument to Daylesford's most famous son, the empire builder, Warren Hastings.

Recommended Reading

Our Bill. Frederick Grisewood. Harrop (1934-1950).

The World Goes By. Frederick Grisewood, Secker & Warburg (1952).

Nearby Strolls

The Birdwatching Don: William Warde Fowler at Kingham (p46)

Guest at the Rectory: Jane Austen at Adlestrop (p40).

The Birdwatching Don
William Warde Fowler at Kingham

Distance: 3 miles

Location: Kingham. The village lies off the B4450, 4 miles SW of Chipping Norton.

Park and Start: Between the church and Cozens Lane, at the southern end of the village. (OS Landranger Sheet 163. GR 259238).

Terrain: Almost entirely along footpaths and bridleways, some of which can be extremely muddy, waterlogged even, during winter or following prolonged rainfall. Level throughout.

Refreshments: Mill Hotel, Plough Inn (both in Kingham). King's Head, Bledington.

Route

➤ From the starting point, walk towards the church. Just beyond the lychgate, a gated footpath cuts off a dangerous corner. From the second gate, turn right along the pavement to reach the footpath to Bledington, signposted at the junction with New Road.

➤ Follow the footpath to reach the gated crossing over the Paddington-Hereford railway line. Cross with care and turn right, parallel with the line, to enter a large field over a stile. This is Coxmoor, the meadow in which Warde Fowler recorded some of his most memorable bird observations.

➤ From the stile, turn half left towards the right-hand corner of the hedge ahead. This is the boundary of the former osier bed, in which Warde Fowler discovered a small colony of rare marsh warblers in the 1890s. Cross a plank bridge spanning a ditch and continue to cross the footbridge over the River Evenlode, leaving Oxfordshire to enter Gloucestershire.

➤ From the bridge, keep straight on for 40 metres to cross a stile in the hedge on the right. The route then keeps another hedge on the left across Coxsmoor, to reach a stile in a fence close by the river bank.

➤ Continue, still with a hedge on the left. Pass through a gate between two large willows to cross a stile in a hedge. The next section of the riverside path may be waterlogged, especially after winter rains and

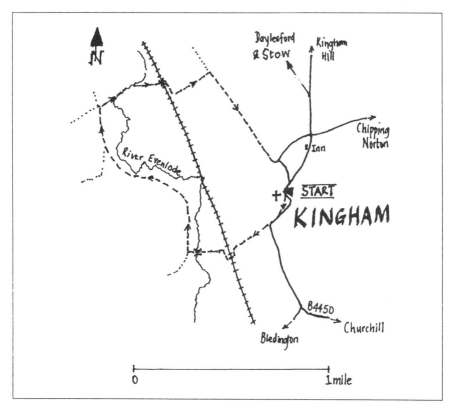

even at other times it is sometimes necessary to make detours to avoid the marshy ground.

➤ Leaving the wet ground behind, the route crosses two more stiles before joining the Bledington-Oddington bridleway, an ancient tree-lined track, sections of which can be muddy. Turn right and follow the track for about 350 metres to reach a handgate on the right, opposite a field gate.

➤ Cross a field to go over a gated bridge. Turn left along the river bank for about 30 metres and then keep the same line to go through a gate. The route continues over another field, climbing to cross a railway bridge.

➤ Beyond the bridge, the diverted route turns right and follows the field edge round two sides to reach a hedged track. Turn right back to Kingham.

➢ After swinging to the left by a lime tree, the route forks. For the more direct way back to the start, turn right along Cozens Lane. To see the rest of the village, keep straight on along West Street before turning right between two greens along Church Street and so back to the start.

Literary Connection

William Warde Fowler (1847-1921) was an Oxford don who took up bird watching as a form of relaxation at a time when to most people, birds existed merely to be killed for sport or for food, their bodies being stuffed for decoration and their eggs displayed in collectors' cabinets.

First in his strolls in the Oxford parks, then over many years weekending and eventually living permanently in Kingham, Fowler learnt to identify birds by sight and sound and to study their behaviour in much the same way as had that great 18th century naturalist, Gilbert White of Selborne. Like White, he left to posterity a detailed and well-written account of his discoveries, first in *A Year with the Birds* and later in a wide-ranging volume dealing with all aspects of his adopted village, entitled *Kingham Old and New*.

Kingham

Among the reminders of Fowler to be seen on the stroll are his house (standing back from Church Street and partly obscured by other houses) opposite the starting point, his simple grave (shared with his sister) near the church porch and Coxsmoor meadow, together with its now-overgrown osier bed, in which Fowler recorded a breeding colony of marsh warblers, a bird on which he was at that time the greatest living authority.

Recommended Reading

A Year with the Birds. W. Warde Fowler. Blackwells & Macmillan (numerous editions).

Kingham Old and New. W.Warde Fowler. Blackwells . 1913.

Warde Fowler's Countryside. ed. Gordon Ottewell. Severn House. 1985.

Nearby Strolls

A Broadcaster's Boyhood: Freddy Grisewood at Daylesford (p43)

Guest at the Rectory: Jane Austen at Adlestrop (p40)

Creator of 'The Countryman': J.W. Robertson Scott at Idbury (p50)

Creator of 'The Countryman'
J.W. Robertson Scott at Idbury

Distance: 2 miles

Location: Idbury. The village lies off the A424, midway between Stow-on-the-Wold and Burford.

Park and Start: Although the stroll commences by the Manor, J.W. Robertson Scott's former home, parking is difficult nearby, as indeed it is anywhere in this tiny village. Perhaps the best place is by the churchyard wall, a short distance along the Kingham road. (OS Landranger Sheet 163. GR 236200).

Terrain: Almost entirely along footpaths and bridleways, which may be muddy after rain. Gentle gradients throughout.

Refreshments: New Inn, Nether Westcote. King's Head, Bledington.

Route

➤ From the tall, distinctive Tudor manor house, with its quotation from Virgil: 'O more than happy countryman, if he but knew his good fortune', over the door, walk along the Kingham road past the church. Opposite the next building, the former school, follow the bridleway sign through a handgate.

➤ Fork to the left along a track and go through another gate immediately on the right. Descend a field to pass through yet another gate, the post of which bears a blue (bridleway) waymark, indicating left.

➤ Follow this bridleway, with a hedge on the left. Wide views now open up. Ahead lie Bruern Woods and the Evenlode Valley, while away to the right, beyond the village of Fifield, the conspicuous landmark of Blackheath Clump (known locally as 'The Cradle') dominates the scene.

➤ At the point where the hedge on the left ends at a field corner, continue straight ahead along the wide grassy track. On passing through a gap in a hedge at the approach to woodland (Herbert's Heath), aim for the right-hand corner of the wood.

➤ At this point, waymarks on a white-topped post indicate a choice of routes. Follow the direction of the right-hand yellow arrow, aiming for the left-hand corner of a clump of woodland. Idbury, and especially the manor and church, provide an appealing view from here.

➤ Beyond the woodland corner, the route maintains a virtually straight course to pass through a hedge gap (marker post). Cross a gently sloping field along a somewhat indistinct path to reach yet another marker post.

➤ Instead of crossing the plank bridge, follow the yellow arrow to the right, keeping the tree-lined stream on the left as far as a stiled foot-bridge.

➤ Cross the stream here and follow the yellow arrow to the right over a field. Beyond a stile, the route keeps another stream on the left and with the Manor ahead, advances to pass through a gate in a hedge.

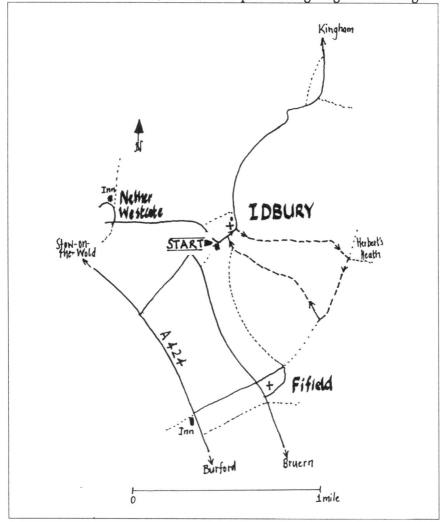

➤ Beyond the gate, continue up a field to cross a stiled footbridge. In the next field, climb to go over a stile by a gate.

➤ Avoid a spring in the last field, from which a final stile leads to a lane. Follow this to reach the village street and the start.

Other features of interest: Two contrasting memorials can be seen in the churchyard. That marking the grave of Sir Benjamin Baker (1840-1907) is an elaborate representation of his engineering feats, he having been responsible for the construction of the first Aswan Dam, the Forth Bridge and the Bakerloo Line. Close by, in the churchyard wall, is the simple bird bath memorial to Elspet Robertson Scott, wife of the founder of 'The Countryman' magazine.

A further memorial is set in the wall in front of the former village school. This is in remembrance of Jessie Jones, a former headmistress, and was placed there by public subscription at the suggestion of J.W. Robertson Scott.

Literary Connection

J.W. Robertson Scott, author, editor and authority on rural affairs, was sixty when, assisted by his wife, he founded 'The Countryman' quarterly magazine at his home, Idbury Manor. It was not until 1947, when he reached 80, that he finally relinquished the editorship and although the magazine then moved to Burford, he continued to contribute to its pages until a few years before his death, aged 96, in 1963.

Robertson Scott loved the Cotswolds and spared no effort to protect the region from exploitation in all its forms. He served for many years on Oxfordshire County Council and was actively concerned with fostering local community spirit, through the provision of good housing, schools and village amenities. Among his many books, *England's Green and Pleasant Land* remains a landmark in rural literature – a hard-hitting indictment against apathy and neglect and especially of the exploitation of the countryside and of the working people living in it.

Recommended Reading

England's Green and Pleasant Land. J.W.Robertson Scott. Cape and Penguin (numerous editions)

Back numbers (pre-1961) of 'The Countryman'.

Nearby Strolls

The Birdwatching Don: William Warde Fowler at Kingham (p46)
Guest at the Rectory: Jane Austen at Adlestrop (p40)
A Broadcaster's Boyhood: Freddy Grisewood at Daylesford (p43)

Cheltenham area

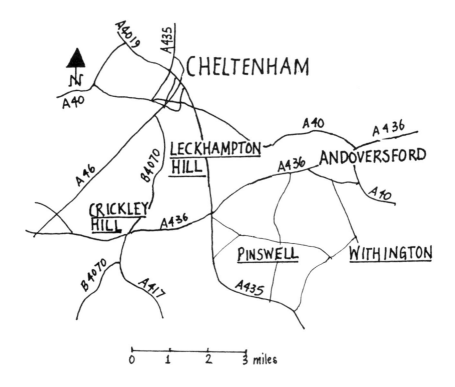

Sketching The Stone
Freda Derrick on Leckhampton Hill

Distance: 1½ miles

Location: Leckhampton Hill. The hill is situated 2 miles south of Cheltenham and is best approached from the B4070 (Cheltenham – Birdlip road).

Park and Start: Car park in disused quarry at Salterley Grange, reached along unclassified road off B4070. Approaching from Cheltenham, watch out for 'Reduce Speed Now' sign and turn left immediately past private drive. The car park is on the left in quarter of a mile. (OS Landranger Sheet 163. GR 946177).

Terrain: Chiefly along level grassy paths, though with a few irregular stony stretches. Finishes with a short downhill length of minor road.

Refreshments: Air Balloon Inn, Crickley Hill (2½ miles SW).

Route

➤ From the car park, return to the approach road and turn left. Climb the short distance to the Cotswold Way footpath sign on the left and follow it onto Leckhampton Hill.

➤ Continue along the escarpment, with its magnificent views westwards to the Malverns and beyond, to arrive at the Devil's Chimney, reached by a signposted path descending for a short distance from the main path in about half a mile. Good views of the overgrown freestone quarries that made such an impression on the youthful Freda Derrick can be had to the right of the Devil's Chimney.

➤ Return to the route and continue to the left along it. Follow the Cotswold Way sign up a gently sloping field. A triangulation pillar soon comes into view on the right.

➤ Pass the pillar on the right. Beyond a conifer clump, ignore a gate on the right. Instead, keep on along an irregular stony path, with a fence on the right, before eventually going through a handgate (blue waymark), also on the right, giving access to a clear footpath.

➤ This path passes between a shallow quarry face on the left and a fence on the right. Beyond a handgate, it reaches a farm lane. Turn left here and then immediately right along the unclassified road leading back to the quarry car park.

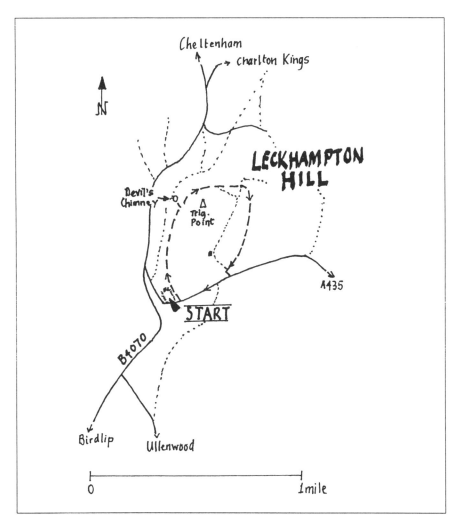

Literary Connection

Freda Derrick (1892-1969) was born and bred in Cheltenham, where her father was chaplain to the workhouse and a keen photographer, especially of a way of country life that was fast disappearing in the face of progress.

Her childhood passion was fossil-hunting in the quarries on nearby Leckhampton Hill and this hobby led her to marvel at the formation and quality of the Cotswold stone itself. Later, through her studies of illus-

Quarry, Leckhampton Hill

tration at the local school of art, she set herself the task of recording traditional rural crafts, travelling considerable distances on her trusty bicycle to interview quarrymen, masons, and anyone she could find who shared her enthusiasm for preserving and perpetuating the best in Cotswold vernacular architecture.

As well as her classic *Cotswold Stone*, Freda Derrick wrote and illustrated several other books, some of which were for children. A comprehensive collection of her drawings can be studied in Cheltenham Art Gallery.

Her regard for Cotswold stone is summarised in the penultimate sentence of her delightful book on the subject: "Cotswold stone building is an art, educates those who work at it, and is a part of our English culture".

Recommended Reading

Cotswold Stone. Freda Derrick. Chapman & Hall. 1948 (republished EP Publishing Ltd. 1974).

Nearby Strolls

The Lady who Lived Alone: Annette MacArthur-Onslow at Pinswell (p62).

A War Poet's Brief Peace: Ivor Gurney on Crickley Hill (p58).

A War Poet's Brief Peace
Ivor Gurney on Crickley Hill

Distance: 1½ miles

Location: Crickley Hill. Now a country park, this promontory of the Cotswold scarp is 4 miles south of Cheltenham and is reached from the B4070, close to its junction with the A436 near the Air Balloon roundabout.

Park and Start: The viewpoint car park on Crickley Hill, close to the visitor centre. (OS Landranger sheet 163. GR 930164).

Terrain: Along clear waymarked paths throughout. The return route is quite steep in places.

Refreshments: The Air Balloon Inn.

Route

➤ From the right-hand extremity of the viewpoint car park, climb steps to reach a kissing gate bearing a Cotswold Way sign (yellow arrow with white dot). This leads across grassland with a beech wood ahead.

➤ By keeping to the left of the woodland, a superb view, much loved by Ivor Gurney, can be enjoyed. On a clear day, and looking from left to right, the main features are the wooded Cooper's Hill, Robinswood Hill (with ski slope), the Forest of Dean uplands, Gloucester (with the cathedral prominent), May Hill (with its top knot of trees), Chosen (or Churchdown) Hill, the Malvern range and Bredon Hill, often likened to a beached whale.

➤ From the point at which the path veers to the right to enter the woodland, a glimpse can be had of Dryhill Farm immediately below, at which Ivor Gurney worked during his brief spell in the Cotswolds following the Great War.

➤ Continue through the woodland. At its end, the path dips before climbing once more. Watch for a red and white marker post on the downward slope and turn sharply to the left by it.

➤ Follow this lower path as far as a fork with another similarly coloured marker post indicating left. Instead of following this, continue along the lower path. Cross a stile alongside a gate and continue to pass through another gate leading to a surfaced lane.

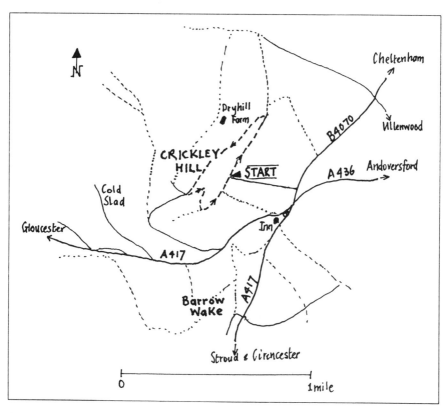

> Keep to the left along this lane and climb a short way to reach a junction with another lane. At this point, turn sharp left to pass through a hand gate and back into the country park.

> Follow the wide main path as far as a light brown and white marker post, indicating a path on the right.

> Take this path, which climbs steadily, with steps in places, to reach a sharp left-hand bend.

> A short diversion to the right can be made at this point to see a prominent stone called the Devil's Table.

> To complete the stroll, turn left. A restored stone wall now appears on the right. Here, the Cotswold Way divides. For the best views, follow the Way's north route, passing the viewing platform overlooking the archaeological excavation site on the right and so back to the start.

Crickley Hill from Barrow Wake

Literary Connection

The prominent hilltop of Crickley was a lifelong passion of Ivor Gurney, the Gloucester-born poet and composer, whose tragic life was cut short by tuberculosis at the age of 47 in 1937. Gurney's musical ability, revealed while a chorister at Gloucester cathedral, developed early both in composition and poetry and eventually won him a place at the Royal College of Music.

A harrowing time as a soldier in the Great War, during which he was gassed, interrupted his studies, however, and contributed to a mental breakdown. This resulted in his being committed to a mental hospital in Kent, where he was to spend the last 15 years of his life.

It was during that brief period between war service and entry into the asylum that Ivor Gurney produced much of his finest work. During this time too, he spent several months labouring at Dryhill Farm, 'under the shadow of the great rise of Crickley', living in an almost derelict farm cottage, and escaping from the drudgery whenever he could to feed his tormented mind on the beauty of his beloved Gloucestershire as seen from the heights of Crickley Hill.

Recommended Reading
Collected Poems of Ivor Gurney (ed. P.J. Kavanagh) O.U.P.1992.
The Ordeal of Ivor Gurney Michael Hurd. O.U.P 1978
A range of leaflets and self-guides to Crickley Hill are available at the visitor centre.

Nearby Strolls
Sketching The Stone: Freda Derrick on Leckhampton Hill (p54).
The Lady Who Lived Alone: Annette Macarthur Onslow at Pinswell (p62).

The Lady who Lived Alone
Annette Macarthur-Onslow at Pinswell

Distance: 2½ miles

Location: Pinswell (merely a plantation and two houses – not signposted) lies between Upper Coberley and Colesbourne. The starting point for the stroll is best reached from the A435 by either of two minor roads (both signposted Upper Coberley), south of the A435/A436 junction at Seven Springs.

Park and Start: The junction of two minor roads above Upper Coberley. Park on verge. (OS Landranger Sheet 163. GR 981160).

Terrain: Along tracks and bridleways, which may be muddy after rain. Generally flat but with one short climb.

Refreshments: The Hungry Horse, Seven Springs (1 mile NW). The Green Dragon, Cockleford (1½ miles SW). The Colesbourne Inn, Colesbourne (3 miles SE).

Route

➢ From the junction (Upper Coberley signpost), walk along the lane towards Withington, passing a cottage on the right. In about 70 metres go through a gateway on the right and follow a bridleway climbing towards Mercombe Wood.

➢ The bridleway passes through the wood to emerge at a cottage, standing at the junction of two tracks. This is the "Round House" once a private toll-house on the old Cirencester-Cheltenham road, and featured in Annette Macarthur's book.

➢ Keep straight on, passing the cottage on the right. An avenue of stately beeches lines the route, with delightful views westward across the Churn Valley. These can be enjoyed at leisure from a seat erected in memory of a Cotswold Voluntary Warden who knew and loved this area for over 40 years.

➢ On the left of the bridleway and partly sheltered by giant beeches can be seen all that remains of Norbury Iron-Age hill fort. This dates from about 500 BC and once enclosed about eight acres. Ploughing has reduced it to a fragment of bank with a shallow outer ditch.

➢ Descend, with a wall on the left. At a right-hand bend, follow the track with a wood now on the left.

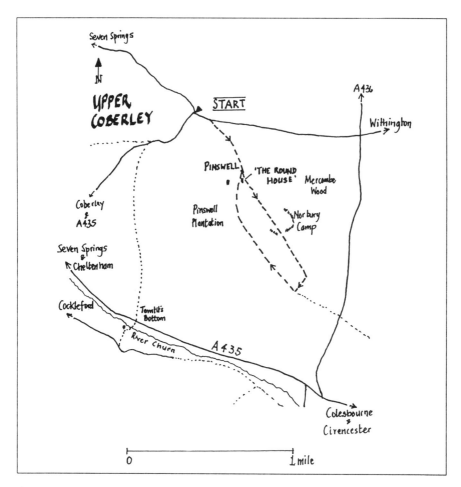

➤ On reaching a junction of tracks, turn right (private road sign) along a
well-surfaced bridleway leading back to the Round House. Retrace
steps to the start.

Literary Connection

In 1972, eight years after the end of her three-year sojourn in an isolated
little Cotswold cottage, the Australian artist, Annette Macarthur-Onslow began to weave the notes, diary jottings and sketches she
had made during that time into a book.

That book, finally published in 1975, was entitled *Round House* and
presents an appealing, if idiosyncratic account of life at Pinswell, shar-

ing the woods with badgers and deer, her neighbours, shepherds and gamekeepers.

Her sole companion during this time was a white cat that had belonged to the Round House's former occupant. It was this cat that provided the subject for Annette Macarthur-Onslow's two earlier books for children – *Uhu* and *Minnie* – the former of which was chosen as children's Book of the Year in Australia in 1970.

Although *Round House* gives essentially a personalised and largely light-hearted picture of life in this remote corner of the Cotswolds, the author provides a welcome touch of authenticity by referring by name to local features that provided her with rich impressions on her walks – Norbury Camp, Mercombe Wood, Needlehole, Cockleford, and so on.

She also researched the derivation of the name Pinswell from a book of 1803: – "Pen – the top and well – a spring of water, descriptive of its situation at the top of a hill, and a continual spring of water descending from it."

Recommended Reading

Round House. Annette Macarthur-Onslow. Collins. 1975.

Nearby Strolls

A War Poet's Brief Peace: Ivor Gurney on Crickley Hill (p58).

Sketching the Stone: Freda Derrick on Leckhampton Hill (p54).

The Rural Rider
William Cobbett at Withington

Distance: 1¼ miles

Location: Withington. The village lies midway between the A40 and the A435, 6 miles SE of Cheltenham.

Park and Start: As near as possible to the church, from which the stroll begins. (O.S. Landranger Sheet 163. GR 031156).

Terrain: A mix of footpath and road walking, with one short climb towards the end of the stroll.

Refreshments: The Mill Inn, the King's Arms Inn.

Route

➤ From the junction by the churchyard and opposite the school, walk down the lane towards the Old Rectory. On reaching the gate pillars, follow the public footpath sign on the right.

➤ Pass beneath two low bridges and continue to reach a third, higher bridge, which formerly carried the railway linking Andoversford Junction with Cirencester.

➤ Beyond this bridge, a kissing-gate gives access to a field. Keep a fence on the left for a short distance to reach a stile on the right. Cross this and go over a field.

➤ The route continues over a footbridge, which leads into another, smaller field. Leave this through a gate straight ahead and pass between fences and by stables to reach a road along a gravelled drive.

➤ Turn right. Pass a road on the left,

Withington church

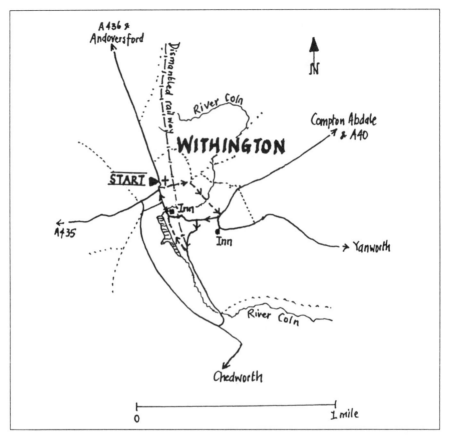

along which can be seen The King's Head Inn, and continue as far as the next turn on the same side, Woodbridge Lane.

➤ This narrow lane climbs at first and soon swings to the right. Eventually, however, it reverts to its former course and dips beneath the shady, fern-clad former railway embankment to reach the remains of a railway bridge.

➤ Immediately beyond this bridge, turn sharp right in front of the aptly-named Riverside Cottage and follow the signposted footpath alongside the Coln.

➤ Cross a stile by a gate and continue, eventually with a fence on the left, to pass between a house and an out building, down steps, and across a paved courtyard to reach a road opposite The Mill Inn.

➤ Turn left, cross the Coln, and climb the hill back to the start.

Literary Connection

It was in September 1826 that the journalist and politician William Cobbett set off on his *Rural Ride* from Worcestershire back to his home county of Hampshire. From Tewkesbury – 'a good substantial town' – the outspoken traveller passed through Cheltenham, a place he loved to hate, before continuing his ride along the Coln valley towards Fairford.

As always, it is the descriptions of the farming practices that are of the most interest to the modern reader. And although Cobbett found the treeless open Cotswolds ugly, he conceded that 'even this wold has many fertile dells in it, and sends out, from its highest parts, several streams, each of which has its pretty valley'.

Such a valley was of course that of the River Coln, and we learn from his account that Cobbett lingered for some time in Withington, the largest village along the upper reaches of this river. From Cheltenham and Dowdeswell, his approach must have been made along the 2½ mile stretch of straight road, then a mere seven years old, which had been constructed following the enclosure of Withington's open fields and entered the village near the church. After likening this church to a small cathedral, Cobbett went on to lament at the decayed state of 'this once populous village', in which he found 'several lanes , crossing each other, which must have been streets formerly. There is a large open space where the principal streets meet ... (and) ...two large, old, roomy houses, with gateways into back parts of them'.

Allowing for Cobbett's tendency to exaggerate rural decay in the interests of political points-scoring, it is interesting both to compare the Withington he knew with the one we see today and to try to identify the present layout of the village from his description. It should be noted that the Andoversford – Cheltenham railway which until it became a victim of Dr Beeching's 'axe' in 1962, was a dominant feature of Withington, came and went in the years between Cobbett's visit and our own time.

Recommended Reading

Rural Rides, Volume 2. William Cobbett

Nearby Strolls

A War Poet's Brief Peace: Ivor Gurney on Crickley Hill (p58)
Sketching the Stone: Freda Derrick on Leckhampton Hill (p54).

Burford and Lechlade area

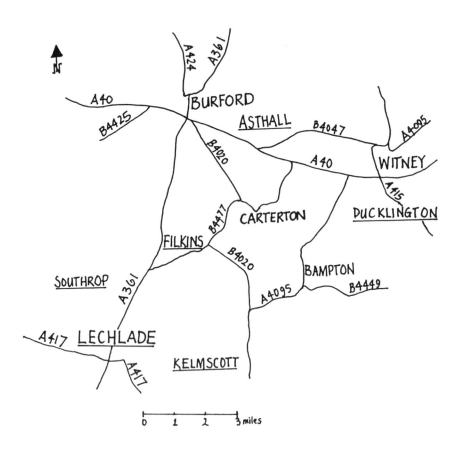

Hons and Rebels
Nancy and Jessica Mitford at Asthall

Distance: 3 miles

Location: Asthall. The village lies 1 mile north of the A40, 2½ miles east of Burford.

Park and Start: Near the church. (O/S Landranger sheet 163. GR 288113).

Terrain: Along field paths, which may be muddy after rain, and minor roads. A few gentle climbs only.

Refreshments: Swan Inn, Swinbrook. Maytime Inn, Asthall

Route

➤ From the church, walk through the village. Turn left at the junction by the inn and continue to cross the bridge spanning the Windrush.

➤ Cross the stile on the left immediately after the bridge and follow the footpath to Swinbrook (good views can be had of Asthall church and manor). Cross a stile in a hedge.

➤ In the next field, keep a wall on the right to reach a double stile. Beyond this, cross a third field to arrive at the southern extremity of Swinbrook via a wall stile, opposite the Swan Inn.

➤ Turn right and follow the winding road. Ignore a right turn and continue to reach a tiny green. The church is ahead on the left. Enter the churchyard through a gate by the 30mph sign.

➤ The grave of David and Sydney Freeman-Mitford, Nancy and Jessica's parents, is away to the right, behind the war memorial. Pamela Jackson's (nee Mitford) grave is by the fence to the right of the church tower. Nancy and Unity's graves are on the right of the path leading towards the gate to the Widford footpath.

➤ To extend the stroll to Widford, go through the handgate at the far left-hand corner of the churchyard and turn right along the walled footpath, which leads in to a field.

➤ The little church of St. Oswald's can be seen standing alone in the fields, to the right of the footpath. The mounds nearby are all that remain of the former village. Beyond, away to the right, stands Widford Manor.

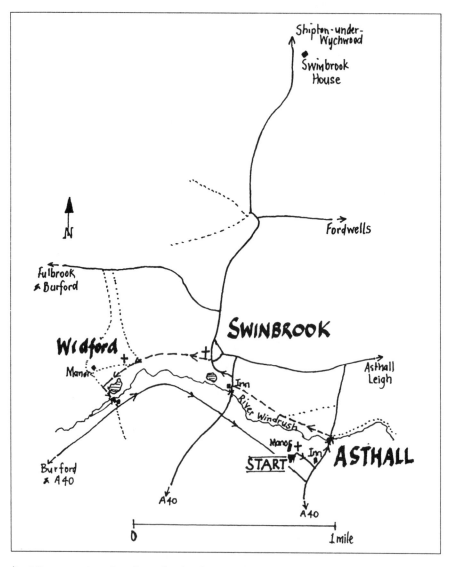

➤ After passing the church, the footpath continues to reach a lane. Turn
left, cross the Windrush, and climb to the T-junction.

➤ Turn left and follow the minor road back to Asthall. The church is
along the lane on the left at the top of a gentle slope. A good view of
the early 17th century Manor House can be had from the churchyard.

Note: Swinbrook House, built by Nancy and Jessica's father and to which the Mitfords moved after leaving Asthall, stands 1½ miles to the north of Swinbrook village and can be glimpsed on the right of the road to Shipton-under-Wychwood.

Literary Connection

It is difficult today to reconcile the two quiet villages of Asthall and Swinbrook with the eventful and at times tempestuous lives of two sisters who wrote of their girlhood spent in this corner of Oxfordshire in the years following the First World War.

Nancy and Jessica Mitford were the daughters of David Free-man-Mitford, the second Lord Redesdale, and his wife Sydney. Together with brother Tom and four sisters – Pamela, Diana, Unity and Deborah – they lived at the early 17th century Asthall Manor from 1919 until 1926, when they moved to the newly-built Swinbrook House, a short distance away.

Nancy (1904-1973) was the oldest of the so-called 'Mitford Girls' and like many novelists, drew extensively on her own life in her numerous fictional works, but especially in her later and most successful novels *The Pursuit of Love*, and *Love In A Cold Climate*. Her father, in particular

The Mitford graves, Swinbrook church

provided her with an outstandingly memorable comic character and the eccentric lifestyle in which she grew up served her well in her search for background material.

Jessica (1917-1996) was an even more colourful character who reacted to the fascist leanings of her sisters Diana and Unity by embracing communism. In her autobiographical *Hons and Rebels*, she presents a delightfully humorous picture of family life, first at Asthall and later at Swinbrook, and like Nancy, makes full use of the bizarre attitudes and prejudices displayed by her father, and to a lesser degree, by her mother, in their dealings with the complexities of daily life.

Recommended Reading

In Pursuit of Love. Nancy Mitford, Hamish Hamilton 1945.

Love In A Cold Climate. Nancy Mitford. Hamish Hamilton 1949.

Hons and Rebels. Jessica Mitford. Victor Gollancz 1960.

The House of Mitford. Jonathan Guinness & Catherine Guinness. Hutchinson 1984.

Nearby Strolls

The Jubilee Boy: George Swinford at Filkins (p76)

Local Girl Who Made Good: Mollie Harris at Ducklington (p73).

Local Girl who Made Good
Mollie Harris at Ducklington

Distance: 2 miles

Location: Ducklington. The village lies off the A415, 1 mile south of Witney.

Park and Start: Near the church, at the southern end of the village. (OS Landranger Sheet 164. GR 359077).

Terrain: Chiefly along tracks and footpaths which can be muddy after rain. Level throughout.

Refreshments: Bell Inn, Strickland Arms.

Route

➤ From the north side of the church, walk along Back Lane. This soon becomes a track, leading to a bridge spanning an arm of the River Windrush.

➤ Continue to a T-junction of tracks. The gate opposite leads into Ducklington's famous fritillary meadow (open to the public on the last Sunday in April).

➤ Turn left. Eventually a yellow waymark indicates that the route passes between a fence and a hedge and continues as far as a stile alongside a gate on the left. Cross this stile and another, 60 metres ahead in a fence.

➤ Go over a long field, aiming for the right-hand tree in a row of willows. The path now crosses two stiles and follows the Windrush to a bridge.

➤ Cross the bridge and turn right along the gravel path into Rushey Meade Nature Reserve, with a lake (excellent for bird watching) on the left and the river on the right at first.

➤ The route eventually swings to the left to pass between the lake and the A40. On reaching a notice board, turn left and then immediately right over a footbridge to reach a surfaced path.

➤ Follow this path as far as a footbridge, leading to a grassy expanse dotted with bushes known as the Moors. Cross this back towards the village along a surfaced path with plank bridges at intervals.

➤ Beyond a stiled footbridge, the path crosses wasteland before keep-

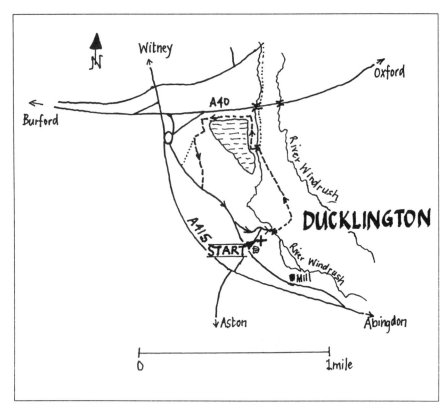

ing garden fences on the right to reach the village street opposite a green.

➤ For a short diversion to see Mollie Harris's childhood home, turn right. Her cottage, now modernised, was the middle one of the row of three directly opposite a garage.

➤ To return to the start, turn left and follow the main street round a series of bends, noticing several old Cotswold-style houses, two excellent examples on the left having 17th century datestones. The pond and former school (now converted into homes) – two village features that figure prominently in Mollie Harris's books – can be seen close to the fine Norman church.

Literary Connection

Although Mollie Harris left her native Oxfordshire village to live at nearby Eynsham in her 30s, it was through her remarkable powers of re-

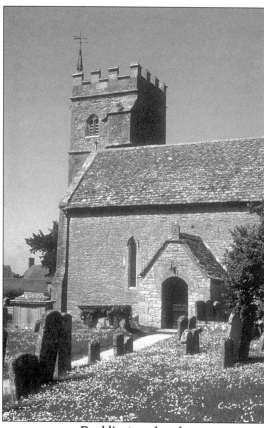

Ducklington church

calling her childhood at Ducklington in the 1920s that she made her reputation as a country writer.

55 years old when her first book, *'A Kind of Magic'*, was published, Mollie embarked on a new phase of life with characteristic zest. Two years later, immediately after completing her second book *'Another Kind of Magic'*, she took up broadcasting. Cast in the role of Martha Woodford in 'The Archers', she played the part for over twenty years, eventually extending her scope to include the seasonal BBC 'Countryside' feature.

More books followed. *Cotswold Privies* was an instant success, to be followed by lavishly produced volumes on the River Windrush and Wychwood Forest. In the meantime, publication of *'The Green Years'* completed her trilogy of Oxfordshire rural life as seen through the eyes of a local girl brought up in poverty in an age gone forever.

Ducklington, in common with the countryside in general, had seen many changes by the time of Mollie Harris's death in 1996. Those changes are still taking place, yet there is much to see in this Cotswold-fringe village made famous by such an able and popular communicator.

Recommended Reading

All Kinds of Magic Mollie Harris O.U.P 1995 (This trilogy contains *A Kind of Magic, The Green Years,* and *Another Kind of Magic*)

The Jubilee Boy
George Swinford at Filkins

Distance: 2½ miles

Location: Filkins. The village lies off the A361, 3½ miles NE of Lechlade.

Park and Start: The stroll commences from outside the museum, at the junction of the village street and Rouse Lane. (OS Landranger Sheet 163. GR 239043). Park by the kerb nearby.

Terrain: A mixture of footpaths, bridleways and minor roads. Flat throughout.

Refreshments: The Lamb Inn and the Five Alls Inn.

Route

➢ Walk along Rouse lane. On the right, bearing a 1929 datestone, is a row of well-designed and constructed council houses built with locally quarried stone by George Swinford and his men with financial support from the local landowner, Sir Stafford Cripps.

➢ At the lane end, continue along the footpath, crossing a stone-slab bridge to enter woodland. At the woodland end, turn right over a stile.

➢ The route keeps woodland on the right. At its end, turn right, and in 20 metres, cross a stone stile on the left.

➢ Cross a scrubby field, with a hedge on the left, to reach a stile in a fence. In the next field, go half right to cross a ditch and pass through a gateway.

➢ Turn left, and after passing the left-hand corner of a garden, swing to the right to reach a road via a gate.

➢ Turn left and walk along the verge for about 300 metres to reach a bridleway (blue arrow) on the right. Follow this on its virtually straight course, as far as a road. (At this point, the stroll can be shortened by turning sharp right along a quiet lane back to Filkins).

➢ To continue the stroll, cross the road to reach Kings Lane. Follow this for almost half a mile, as far as a stile and footpath sign on the right just before a left-hand bend.

➢ Take the direction indicated by the yellow arrow across a field to-

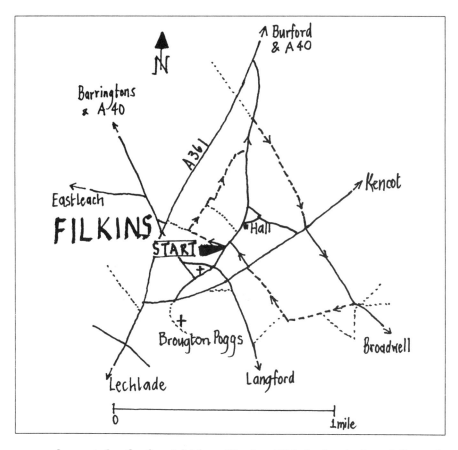

wards a gate by the far right-hand hedge. This hedge is then followed as far as a gate at a junction of paths.

> Turn right here, keeping a hedge on the right, to reach a road. Cross straight over along Hazells Lane, which leads back to the village street. The museum is on the left.

Literary Connection

No-one would have been more surprised to find himself included in a book on literary figures of the Cotswolds than George Swinford. Born and bred in the Oxfordshire village of Filkins, George spent his entire life there, apart from four years as a soldier in the First World War. He was a mason by trade but in a long and active life – he lived to be a hundred – he turned his hand to just about every other occupation associated with building, and his handiwork remains, and will continue to remain, as tangible evidence of his skill with and love of Cotswold stone.

Fortunately, George not only gave a number of interviews to guide-book authors and writers of articles over the years but somehow found time to set down his recollections in an exercise book between 1955 and 1958. These jottings form the nucleus of *Jubilee Boy*, a book about his eventful life, researched and edited by two fellow villagers and published just before his death in 1987.

Jubilee Boy is unique as both a social and historical document. It gives a vivid description of Cotswold village life from late Victorian times , together with an informed account of the part local stone has played in creating the Cotswolds we see today.

Filkins itself bears testimony to the skilful way that the limestone has been put to use over the centuries. Many of the gardens are fenced with giant slabs, known locally as planks, while the village streets and lanes are lined with a range of buildings representing several centuries, and including examples of George's own handiwork in the form of the distinctive council houses in Rouse Lane.

A further reminder of George Swinford is the little museum, housing the many and varied rural bygones he collected over the years. For opening dates, contact Burford Tourist Information Centre.

Recommended Reading

The Jubilee Boy. George Swinford. Edited by Judith Fay and Richard Martin. Filkins Press. 1987.

Nearby Strolls

The Poet's Path: Percy Shelley at Lechlade (p83)

The Craftsman's Corner: William Morris at Kelmscott (p86)

The Scholar and his Church: John Keble at Southrop (p79)

The Scholar and his Church
John Keble at Southrop

Distance: 3 miles
Location: Southrop. The village lies off the A361, 2½ miles north of Lechlade.
Park and Start: Near the Swan Inn in the centre of the village. (OS Landranger Sheet 163. GR 200035).
Terrain: A varied stroll along minor roads and footpaths, which may be muddy after rain. Gentle gradients only.
Refreshments: Swan Inn, Southrop. Victoria Inn, Eastleach Turville.

Route

➤ From the Swan Inn, follow the Filkins signpost down the village street. A short way along on the right stands the Old Vicarage, in the garden of which towers a superb cedar of Lebanon. Together with the ancient yew shading the raised pavement, it bore witness to the meetings between John Keble and his friends that led to the founding of the Oxford Movement.

➤ Beyond the school, and opposite the path leading to Manor Farm and the church, is a stone stile set back from the road between two houses. However, before crossing it (or at the end of the stroll if preferred) it is well worth exploring the village.

➤ Below, on the left is the former corn mill, dating from the 17th century and converted in the 1960s into a delightful private residence surrounded by gardens to match. The path to St Peter's church provides views of the charming 16th century manor house and of a fine barn. Within the ancient church with its distinctive late-Saxon herringbone masonry, is the superbly decorated 12th century font, said to have been discovered by John Keble, walled up near the south doorway.

➤ Resuming the stroll, cross the stone stile and continue over paddocks to enter a large field. Bear half right to cross the River Leach. Turn left immediately beyond the bridge and follow the riverside path to reach a road.

➤ Turn right. In a short distance, cross a stile on the left to reach another

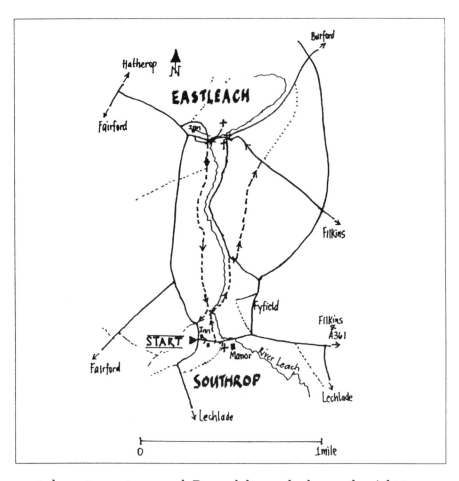

at the entrance to a wood. Beyond, keep a hedge on the right to pass through another small wood.

➤ Cross a footbridge and climb a field to reach a road. Turn left into Eastleach Martin. At a junction, turn left to pass through the church-yard and over Keble's Bridge.

➤ From the bridge, a short detour can be made to Eastleach Turville church, in which a copy of Keble's *A Christian Year* is displayed.

➤ Continue the stroll to reach the war memorial. Turn left here, right by the phone box and left at the next turn beyond. Now keep to the right to reach a public footpath sign indicating left by a cottage.

➤ Climb a narrow path to a stile leading into a field. Cross to another stile. Keep a line of trees and bushes on the left to pass through a gateway.

➤ From this point, go half right over a field towards a solitary house. Cross a footbridge, followed by a stile. Turn left along a wall to pass the house.

➤ Cross the drive to reach a stile leading into a field. Climb towards the left-hand extremity of the hedge on the right. Beyond, aim towards a dovecote to reach a gate in the field corner.

➤ A track leads to a road. Turn left back into Southrop. The Swan Inn is on the left.

Literary Connection

Southrop, together with its near neighbours, the Eastleaches, comprises 'Keble Country'. This noteworthy family lived at Grey's Court, in the village, during the 17th century; one of their number, Thomas, is commemorated in the church by a monument bearing his coat of arms and dated 1670. Today, the Kebles are best remembered through John (1792-1866). Born at Fairford, John Keble was a brilliant scholar at Oxford, where he became a tutor and was later appointed Professor of Poetry. However, his ideal seems to have been to be a country clergyman

Keble's bridge, Eastleach

and after taking holy orders, he became curate to his father, serving in that capacity at Coln St Aldwyns, the Eastleaches and Southrop.

It was during his time of residence at Southrop vicarage (1823-25) that Keble, together with his friends Hurrell Froude, Isaac Williams and Robert Wilberforce, prepared the way for the founding of the Oxford Movement, which was to transform the 19th century Anglican church.

Keble's collection of sacred poetry *The Christian Year*, also appeared at this time. Although seldom read today, some of these poems became popular hymns, including *New Every Morning* and *Blessed Are The Pure In Heart*. A copy of *The Christian Year* can be seen in Eastleach Turville church. The delightful stone footbridge over the Leach, connecting the Eastleach villages is still known as Keble's Bridge. Although John Keble left the Cotswolds in 1836 to become vicar of Hursley in Hampshire, his name remains indelibly imprinted on the region. Some idea of his reputation as a scholar is indicated by the founding of Keble College in Oxford in his memory in 1869.

Nearby Strolls

The Jubilee Boy: George Swinford at Filkins (p76).

The Poet's Path: Percy Shelley at Lechlade (p83).

The Poet's Path
Percy Shelley at Lechlade

Distance: 1½ miles

Location: Lechlade. The town stands at the junction of the A417 and the A361, 8½ miles south of Burford.

Park and Start: In or near the market place in the town centre. (OS Landranger Sheet 163. GR 215995).

Terrain: A mix of pavement, surfaced path and field path. Level throughout.

Refreshments: Choice of inns in town. The Trout Inn at St John's Bridge.

Route

➤ From the market place, follow the paved path to the left of the church. This is known as Shelley's Walk and a short extract from his poem *A Summer Evening Churchyard. Lechlade, Gloucestershire*, is inscribed on a stone in the wall on the left.

➤ The path passes through what must surely be one of the most appealing churchyards in Gloucestershire, with its fine yews and beeches and its varied collection of tombstones, the oldest decipherable ones dating back to the late 17th century. To the right stands an elegant early 18th century house complete with gazebo, one of several raised summerhouses to be found locally and from which ladies of the period could watch passers-by.

➤ On leaving the churchyard, cross the school approach road and continue through a kissing gate and along a surfaced path, complete with stiles, which leads to the A417 at its junction with the Kelmscott road.

➤ Turn right to cross the Thames over St John's Bridge. Before the bridge is the Trout Inn, known formerly as St John Baptist's Head. It is said to stand on the site of the almshouse of a priory and to have been built to house the workmen engaged in building the first stone bridge, which replaced a wooden structure around 1220.

➤ On the left of the bridge parapet can be seen the confluence of the Thames with its tributary, the Leach, which gave its name to Lechlade.

➤ Watch for a handgate and steps on the right immediately beyond the

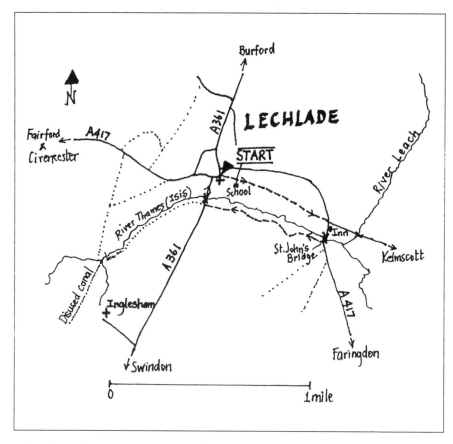

bridge. These give access to the Thames Path at St John's Lock, the highest on the river. Notice the statue of Old Father Thames by the lock keeper's house.

➤ This was created for the Great Exhibition of 1851 and stood originally at the source of the Thames before being moved here to protect it from vandalism.

➤ Follow the Thames Path through the handgate and along the river bank to Halfpenny Bridge, dating from 1792 and with its former toll cottage still in place. Pass under the bridge and climb the steps to the left to reach the A361.

➤ Cross the bridge and continue to the T-junction. The market place is on the right.

Literary Connection

It was in the late summer of 1815 that the poet Percy Bysshe Shelley, then aged 23, arrived at Lechlade with his friends Mary Godwin (whom he married in the following year), Thomas Love Peacock and Charles Clairemont after rowing up the Thames from Windsor.

According to Peacock, Shelley suffered from listlessness at the start of the voyage but after being persuaded to give up his diet of bread and butter in favour of peppered mutton chops, he rallied to such a degree that soon he 'had the ruddy, healthy complexion of the autumn upon his countenance'. He 'rowed vigorously, was cheerful, merry and over-flowing with animal spirits' – so much so that he declared his intention of rowing to the source of the Thames. This the party failed to do how-ever, and instead, stayed for two nights at the New Inn before rowing back to Windsor. Whatever the state of Shelley's spirits, Lechlade churchyard at eventide exerted an irresistible attraction, the result be-ing a Gothic dirge that with its allusions to 'twilight, unbeloved of men', 'the stars and clouds of night', and 'the dead sleep-ing in their sepulchres' could well have set the scene for his future wife's famous novel, *Frankenstein*, which appeared three years later.

It was not until 1968 that the path through the churchyard was officially designated 'Shelley's Walk' by the insertion of a stone bearing a fragment of the poem into the wall opposite the church door.

Shelley's Walk, Lechlade

Recommended Reading

A Summer Evening Churchyard. Lechlade, Gloucestershire. (Included in Shelley's collected poems).

Nearby Strolls

The Craftsman's Corner: William Morris at Kelmscott (p86).

The Jubilee Boy: George Swinford at Filkins (p76).

The Scholar and his Church: John Keble at Southrop (p79).

The Craftsman's Corner
William Morris at Kelmscott

Distance: 2 miles

Location: Kelmscott. The village lies midway between the A417 and A4095, 2½ miles east of Lechlade.

Park and Start: At the northern end of the village, near the church. (OS Landranger Sheet 163. GR 250994)

Terrain: Along minor roads and footpaths, which may be muddy after rain. Level throughout.

Refreshments: Plough Inn.

Manor opening times: Wednesday (1 April-30 Sept) 11am-1pm and 2pm-5pm and the third Saturday in each month (April-Sept), 2pm-5pm (Phone 01367 252486 for confirmation and admission charges.)

Route

➤ This begins at the church. William Morris's grave, with its ridge-shaped stone supported on blocks, is in a secluded corner to the right of the churchyard gate. Emerging from the gate, turn left. Pass the first right turn and continue as far as a second, at a sharp left-hand bend.

➤ This lane passes Manor Farm, one of several handsome farmhouses in the village and dating from the early 18th century. Notice the turreted and gabled dovecote close by.

➤ On reaching a junction, turn right. A short distance on the left stands Morris Cottages, alongside which are two estate cottages, which, like their neighbours, were built in memory of her husband by Jane Morris.

➤ Pass the Plough Inn and the base of an ancient cross. Beyond, turn left along a lane signposted as a public footpath to Buscot Lock. Keep to the right between walls and continue between hedges as far as a white marker post.

➤ Turn left, as indicated by the yellow waymark, and follow the footpath along the field edge to its end. Cross two footbridges and a stile and continue over a field as indicated by another waymark, with a fence on the right.

➤ On reaching the Thames Path at a handgate, do not pass through. In-

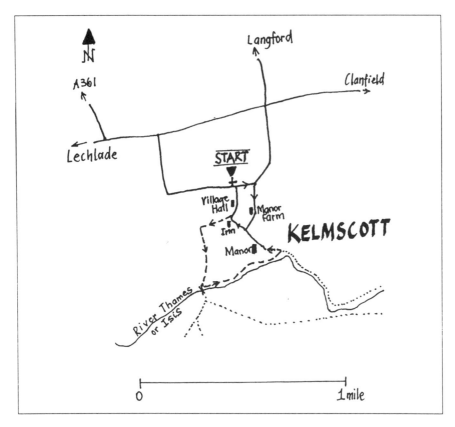

stead, turn left along the river bank and continue, via a gate and a footbridge, to reach a lane.

➤ Turn left, leaving the river. After rounding a bend, Kelmscott Manor, dating from about 1570, comes into view. Beyond, at the junction passed earlier, retrace steps to the inn and continue past the village

Kelmscott Manor

hall, with its stone slab fence, to reach a junction. The church is on the left.

Literary Connection

Between 1871 and his death in 1896, the artist ,craftsman, poet and visionary William Morris spent much of his life at the lovely 16th century house known as Kelmscott Manor, which he described to a friend as 'a heaven on earth' and which provided him with the ideal environment in which to pursue his literary, craftmanship and political interests away from the demands of his London existence.

This is not to say that Morris's Kelmscott days comprised uninterrupted serenity. He had entered into a joint tenancy of the Manor with his fellow pre-Raphaelite, the poet Dante Gabriel Rossetti, whose love affair with Morris's wife Jane placed an almost unbearable strain on the marriage for some time before Rossetti finally departed.

In 1880 and again in the following year, Morris, together with his wife, their two daughters and a small party of friends, sailed in their boat, 'The Ark', up the Thames from Hammersmith to Kelmscott, a journey Morris relished to such a degree that he described it in detail in his fictional *News from Nowhere*. At Kelmscott, he was never happier than when wandering along the river bank and quiet lanes, savouring the flora and fauna and collecting natural materials for making into dyes or studying the mosaic of the vegetation, later to be reproduced in textile designs.

Apart from his grave in the churchyard and the Manor, other associations with Morris seen on the stroll include the Memorial Hall, built of local stone and completed in 1934 to a design by a disciple of Morris, Ernest Gimson; and the Memorial Cottages, built in 1902 by Philip Webb on the instructions of Morris's widow and embellished with a carving of Morris by George Jack.

Recommended Reading

Selected Writings. William Morris. Nonsuch Press 1946.

Nearby Strolls

The Poet's Path: Percy Shelley at Lechlade (p83).
The Jubilee Boy: George Swinford at Filkins (p76).

Cirencester area

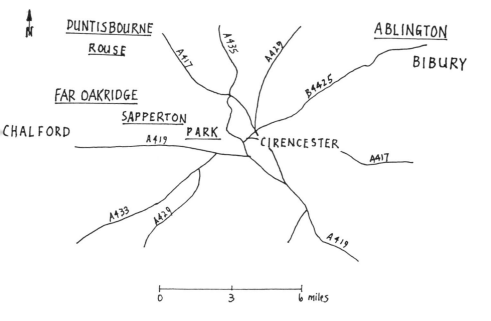

The Curious Traveller
H.J. Massingham at Duntisbourne Rouse

Distance: 3 miles (short option, three-quarters of a mile)

Location: Duntisbourne Rouse. The hamlet lies 4 miles NW of Cirencester and 1 mile west of the A417. If travelling along the A417, follow Duntisbourne Leer signs.

Park and Start: As near as possible to the junction of a through road with the Duntisbourne Abbots – Daglingworth road about 1½ miles from Duntisbourne Leer. (OS Landranger Sheet 163. GR 985059).

Terrain: Chiefly along footpaths and bridleways, with one stretch of minor road walking. Gentle gradients.

Refreshments: The Highwayman, Beechpike, Winstone.

Route

➤ From the junction, walk along the no-through-road into Duntisbourne Rouse hamlet. The beguiling little River Dunt flows over a ford at the foot of the slope. The public footpath leading to the church is on the left before the ford. Notice the scissor-type gate (not in use – a functioning one can be seen to the left of the church).

➤ Leave the churchyard over a stile in the far wall. Pass through woodland and leave over a stile. The path descends a field to a double stile.

➤ In the next field, aim to the left of a derelict barn to cross a stile in a fence.

➤ A short but steep descent leads to a handgate between two barns at the hamlet of Middle Duntisbourne, with another ford to the right.

➤ Turn left and follow the winding lane up to the road. Turn left again.

➤ To return by the short route, follow this road back to the start.

➤ Otherwise in 250 metres, turn right at a bridleway sign. This route swings to the right at a bend and continues for a further three-quarters of a mile to reach the delightful Longhill Road at the northerly limit of Overley Wood, part of Cirencester Park.

➤ Turn left and follow this quiet hedged road for a further three-quarters of a mile, passing Longhill Farm.

➤ Leave the road at a waymarked handgate on the left in a slight hollow. The path passes a small pond immediately on the right before cross-

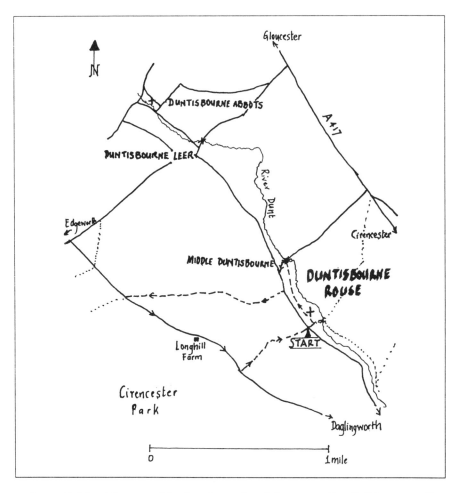

ing a field with a scrubby bank on the right to reach a field gate at the
far right-hand corner.

➤ Beyond this gate keep fenced woodland on the left to reach the starting point through another gate.

Literary Connection

Harold John Massingham (1888-1952) was one of the most respected
and prolific writers on the English countryside during the first half of
the 20th century. In the 1930s he lived for some years near Chipping
Campden and his books on the region - *Wold Without End* (1932),

Cotswold Country (1937) and *Shepherds Country* (1938) – are essential reading for anyone wishing to gain a deeper appreciation of man's influence on the Cotswold landscape from the earliest times.

Massingham was a tireless campaigner against the despoilation of the countryside and in particular, lamented the decline of rural craftsmanship in all its forms. It followed that he never ceased to delight in the simple dignity of old Cotswold buildings, especially churches. One such church was St Michael's, Duntisbourne Rouse, which he re-visited many years after leaving the region and which he described in *The Curious Traveller* as possessing 'the modesty of the cottage-church', its poignant grace making it 'a church of the still, small voice ... The church commands the earth not by pride but the inward sovereignty of meekness'.

Half a century later, this tiny late Saxon/early Norman church still retains the simple appeal that so beguiled Massingham. The gigantic slab-tombs he noted in the sloping churchyard, the distinctive saddle-back tower, and within, the box pews, misericords and medieval wall paintings – all continue to delight the visitor to this unique little church mercifully spared the heavy hand of the Victorian restorer.

Recommended Reading

The Curious Traveller. Collins 1950.

Wold Without End. Cobden-Sanderson. 1932

Cotswold Country. Batsford. 1937

Shepherds Country. Chapman & Hall. 1938

All written by H.J. Massingham.

Nearby Strolls

Poet in the Park: Alexander Pope at Cirencester (p100).

The Roving Craftsman: Norman Jewson at Sapperton (p96).

The Dramatist finds Delight

John Drinkwater at Far Oakridge

Distance: 2¼ miles (short option, three-quarters of a mile)

Location: Far Oakridge. The village lies 4 miles east of Stroud and 2 miles SE of Bisley.

Park and Start: On the roadside verge near the nameboard at the western approach to the village. (OS Landranger Sheet 163. GR 922036).

Terrain: Along quiet roads and a bridleway. Two steepish climbs.

Refreshments: Butcher's Arms, Oakridge Lynch.

Route

➤ From the junction at the western end of the village, follow the Iles Green signpost to the right. Iles Farm, the second substantial house on the left, was for many years the home of the artist Sir William Rothenstein, whose initials, together with those of his wife, can be clearly seen from the road. Also visible are the dates 1614 and 1914, recording the age of the original house and the date of its enlargement and restoration by the celebrated craftsman Norman Jewson.

➤ Continue to a fork. Turn left. On reaching Oakridge Farm, follow the lane as it climbs steeply to the left to reach a small green.

➤ Take the right fork. Winston Cottage, formerly the home of the essayist, critic and caricaturist Max Beerbohm and later of John Drinkwater, dramatist and poet, stands on the right at the next junction. To complete the short option, turn left here and back to the start.

➤ Otherwise, continue along the road ahead, which winds delightfully along woodland fringes and by flora-rich hedgebanks, to reach a junction overlooking Frith House.

➤ Turn left here, up a lane signposted Waterlane and Bisley. A stiffish climb follows. On reaching the next junction, at the hamlet of Waterlane, follow the Oakridge Lynch signpost to the left.

➤ At the next junction, take the bridleway signposted on the left. This leads back to Far Oakridge, opposite the lane walked at the start of the stroll.

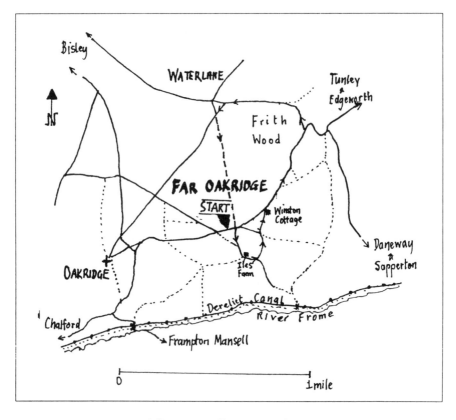

Literary Connection

It was in 1912 that the artist William Rothenstein bought the 17th century Iles Farm at Far Oakridge, a hamlet perched high above the Frome Valley, near Stroud. Soon, a steady stream of artists and literary friends began to visit, including among others the Indian poet Tagore, W.H. Davies, and Max Beerbohm. With the outbreak of war two years later, Rothenstein offered the tenancy of Winston Cottage to Beerbohm, and the essayist lived in the modest cottage throughout the conflict, though never managing to adjust to country life.

Beerbohm's departure in 1918 made way for another celebrated literary tenant, though one to whom the local countryside was 'The most beautiful in England' and who in an essay dedicated to Rothenstein thanked him for 'having found me a corner of your enchanted Cotswold country.' This newcomer was John Drinkwater, poet, dramatist and highly successful manager of the Birmingham Repertory Theatre.

Winston cottage

Drinkwater (1882 – 1937) was no stranger to Gloucestershire, having been actively associated with the so-called 'Muse Colony' of poets centred on the Dymock area during the period leading up to the outbreak of war. (see *A Poet's Patch*. W.W. Gibson at Leddington p126). Now however, he was able to immerse himself in rural life, delighting in exploring the tangle of lanes and footpaths, fetching water from the spring, making friends with his fellow villagers and playing cricket and going fishing with the Rothenstein children, to whom he appeared as a favourite 'uncle'.

Professionally, too, Drinkwater's three years at Winston Cottage was a highly productive period. While residing there he completed his play *Abraham Lincoln*, which was to prove an unqualified success both in England and in the United States, while his poetry and descriptive writing drew deeply on his Cotswold surroundings.

Recommended Reading

Cotswold Characters. John Drinkwater (OUP 1921).

Selected Poems. John Drinkwater (Sidgwick & Jackson 1922).

Nearby Strolls

The Roving Craftsman: Norman Jewson at Sapperton (p96).

The Curious Traveller: H.J. Massingham at Duntisbourne Rouse (p90).

The Poet In The Park: Alexander Pope in Cirencester Park (p100).

The Roving Craftsman
Norman Jewson at Sapperton

Distance: 2¾ miles

Location: Sapperton. The village lies one mile north of the A419, 8 miles east of Stroud.

Park and Start: Along the no-through-road leading past the church. (OS Landranger Sheet 163. GR 948035).

Terrain: An undulating route. Chiefly along footpaths, bridleways and minor roads. The path through Dorvel Wood can be muddy after rain. The one steepish climb is near the end of the stroll.

Refreshments: Bell Inn, Sapperton. Daneway Inn (on route).

Route

➤ From the churchyard gate, turn right and walk along the lower village street, from which delightful views can be enjoyed across the wooded Frome Valley. Turn left up the footpath opposite the school to reach the upper green. The steeply-gabled Batchelor's Court, formerly Norman Jewson's house, stands on the left, with its striking yew topiary work over the gate and in the garden.

➤ Turn right opposite the house and cross the green to reach a crossroads by a lower green. Again turn right, passing the school once more, and continue to reach a lane descending on the left.

➤ Follow this as far as a walled path on the left, which eventually descends to a stile giving access to a field.

➤ The footpath passes a water trough and descends to the right of a large oak to reach another stile. Beyond, it passes above the restored portal of the Thames-Severn Canal tunnel before swinging right along the former towpath. Follow this, with the tiny River Frome on the left, to reach a road bridge at Daneway.

➤ Turn right and right again by the Daneway Inn. In rather less than half a mile, and immediately beyond the drive to Daneway House, which figured prominently in the story of the work of Gimson and the Barnsley brothers as recounted in *By Chance I did Rove*, turn right along a signposted right-of-way into Dorvel Wood.

➤ Keep to the main woodland track for a little over half a mile, as far as a

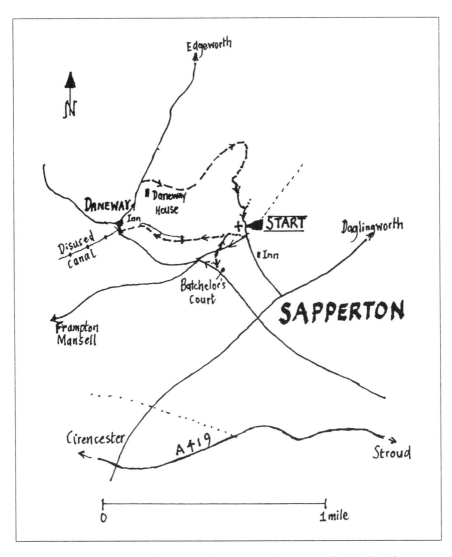

crossways of paths. (A view of Daneway House can be had at the start of this section).

➢ On reaching the crossways, turn right, descending to cross the Frome before climbing to the left by a garden wall to reach a road.

➢ Turn right and follow this narrow sunken road to reach a T-junction. Turn right once more back to Sapperton and the start.

Literary Connection

It was in 1907 that Norman Jewson, a newly-qualified architect, arrived by train at Cirencester in his search for an escape from London. Eager to see for himself the much-praised architecture and scenery of the Cotswolds, he hired a donkey and trap and set out on a journey of discovery, eventually finding his way to Sapperton, where he met the craftsman Ernest Gimson and was invited to join him on a month's trial.

Sapperton church

In his one book, *By Chance I Did Rove,* Jewson describes how this brief period was extended to a lifetime, which he devoted to designing and renovating Cotswold houses, among them the beautiful Tudor Owlpen Manor, near Dursley. But *By Chance I Did Rove* is much more than a mere exercise in autobiography; in it Jewson gives a finely-observed account of the lives and work of Ernest Gimson and of Ernest and Sidney Barnsley, who took as their inspiration the work of William Morris, pioneer of the Arts and Crafts movement. There is gentle humour too in the description of village life and characters, both in Sapperton and further afield.

No visit to Sapperton would be complete without a tour of St Kenelm's church, in the churchyard of which can be seen the graves of Ernest Gimson and the Barnsley brothers. St Kenelm's, though dating from the Norman period, was rebuilt in the 14th century and again early in the time of Queen Anne, by the Atkyns family. Not to be missed in the south transept is the sumptuous tomb of Sir Robert Atkyns, author of *The Ancient and Present State of Gloucestershire,* published soon after his death in 1711 and the first book on the county.

Compared with this, the monument to Norman Jewson, who died in 1975, is a modest affair – the almsbox by the church door.

Recommended Reading

By Chance I Did Rove. Norman Jewson. 1973

Nearby Strolls

The Dramatist finds delight: John Drinkwater at Far Oakridge (p93)

Poet in the Park: Alexander Pope at Cirencester (p100)

The Curious Traveller: H.J. Massingham at Duntisbourne Rouse (p90).

The Poet in the Park

Alexander Pope at Cirencester

Distance: 3 miles

Location: Cirencester Park. The Park entrance is reached from Cecily Hill, off Park Street, on the western edge of Cirencester.

Park and Start: Cecily Hill. (OS Landranger Sheet 163. GR 018022). Restricted parking only on Cecily Hill. Suggest using one of the main car parks.

Terrain: Chiefly along surfaced estate roads and paths, though with stretches of walking over grass, which may be muddy after rain. Level throughout.

Refreshments: Wide choice of inns and teashops in Cirencester.

Route

➢ From the Park gates, walk along the splendid straight Broad Ride. In about 600 metres on the right is the first of several follies scattered across the Park. This is the Hexagon, standing on a plinth and with three of its six arched openings blocked. It was built to Lord Bathurst's own design in 1736.

➢ Continue as far as the end of the surfaced section of Broad Ride. (Note: no dogs are allowed beyond this point).

➢ Keep straight on along what is now a broad grassy ride. Go over a cross track. The small stone pavilion known as Pope's Seat soon appears on the right.

➢ To vary the stroll instead of retracing steps, follow the wide grassy path to the right to reach a surfaced road.

➢ Turn right along this and follow it, keeping Broad Ride on the right, back almost to the end of the surfaced section of Broad Ride.

➢ Just before reaching Broad Ride, turn left and in 20 metres, right, along a woodland path with a ditch on the right.

➢ Follow this path, with Broad Ride still on the right, to reach the Hexagon, passed previously.

➢ Retrace steps along Broad Ride back to Cecily Hill.

Note: The name Cirencester Park applies not only to the parkland but to the early 18th century mansion itself. Unlike most great houses, it

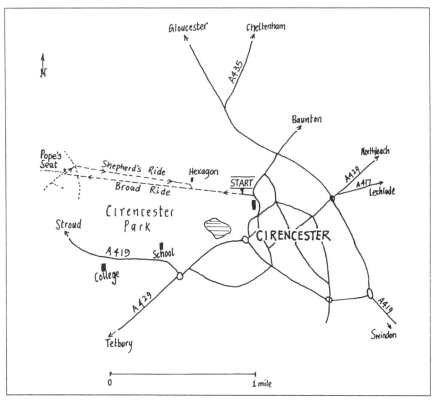

stands on the edge of the town and is partly hidden by a magnificent yew hedge (passed on approach to Cecily Hill). The castle-like building on the right near the Park entrance was built in 1857 as the headquarters of the Royal North Gloucestershire Militia.

Literary Connection

In 1721, the poet Alexander Pope began a working partnership with his patron, Allen, the first Earl Bathurst. Extending over 20 years, this partnership produced what still remains one of the most elegant and extensive areas of parkland in the country offering public access – Cirencester Park.

Born the son of a London merchant in 1688, Pope had a severe illness at the age of 12 and was left a cripple. Despite being only four feet six inches in height and with a delicate constitution, he educated himself and began writing verse, the quality of which soon won praise from such prominent literary contemporaries as Wycherley, Addison and Swift.

Pope's Seat, Cirencester Park

Landscape designing seems a far cry from composing verse but encouraged by his noble patron, Pope threw himself into the planning of Cirencester Park with characteristic zest. With his aim being 'to create the amiable simplicity of unadorned nature', he worked with Earl Bathurst to fashion a landscape of ten long avenues radiating out across the park and incorporating a number of existing woods and copses. In addition, the two friends decided to introduce an assortment of fanciful buildings, or follies, to provide further interest. These included a sham castle, a Gothic lodge, a Doric column surmounted by a statue of Queen Anne, and a small rusticated pavilion named appropriately Pope's Seat.

Although it is with his house and grounds at Twickenham that Alexander Pope is usually associated, Cirencester Park seems to have been almost a second home to him during his lengthy association with the first Earl Bathurst.

Recommended Reading

Cirencester – A History and Guide. Jean Welsford. Sutton. 1987.

Nearby Strolls

The Roving Craftsman: Norman Jewson at Sapperton (p96)
The Curious Traveller: H.J. Massingham at Duntisbourne Rouse (p90)

Squire and Villager

J. Arthur Gibbs at Ablington

Distance: 2½ miles
Location: Ablington. The hamlet lies one mile NW of the B4425 at Bibury.
Park and Start: Near the junction of the Bibury-Winson road with a no-through-road, close to the bridge over the River Coln. (OS Landranger Sheet 163. GR 103077).
Terrain: Along minor roads and field paths, which may be muddy after rain. One steepish road climb near start.
Refreshments: Catherine Wheel Inn, Arlington.

Route

➤ From the bridge over the Coln, with a glimpse of the Manor grounds on the left, walk up to the T-junction. Turn left here, (Barnsley and Cirencester signpost). After a steepish climb, the road levels out and in about three-quarters of a mile, joins the B4425 at a meeting of five ways, Arlington Pike.

➤ Cross straight over to follow a signpost indicating a road used as a public path. (This is in fact a grassy track). At the field end, turn left, in the direction indicated by a public footpath sign.

➤ Go over two stiles and keeping a hedge on the left, continue to cross a traditional Cotswold stone stile.

➤ Beyond this, a wooden stile gives access to a track, which leads back to the B4425 at Arlington. Cross and turn right.

➤ In a short distance, turn left along a no-through-road opposite a telephone box. (A detour can be made from here to visit Bibury and/or the Catherine Wheel inn). Keep to the left at a fork and continue to pass through a handgate.

➤ Climb a stile by a gate and follow a field edge to go over a stone stile.

➤ Cross a surfaced track and go over a field to two more stiles.

➤ Beyond a final stile, the path continues to reach the top of the slope climbed on the outward route.

➤ Retrace steps to the start.

To see Ablington Manor, formerly the home of J. Arthur Gibbs, follow the Bibury road for a short distance. The Manor stands on the right, partly hidden behind a high wall. It dates from 1590 and was built by

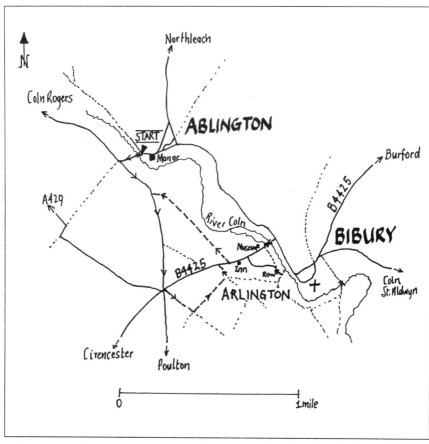

John Coxwell. A little further on, and on the opposite side, stand two
magnificent stone barns, while beyond, near the eastern extremity of
the hamlet, is Ablington House, built in the mid 17th century but with a
novel 19th century addition – gateposts featuring stone lions that once
embellished the Houses of Parliament.

Literary Connection

A Cotswold Village by J. Arthur Gibbs, the young squire of Ablington
during the 1890s, is generally accepted as being the first of the many
fine books written in praise of the region. Gibbs, surprisingly, was not a
Cotswold man. The likelihood is that he discovered the region's charms
while an undergraduate at Oxford; the Swan Hotel at Bibury was a popular rendezvous for such wealthy young men in the 1880s after Bibury's

The River Coln near Ablington

praises had been sung by William Morris. At all events, Gibbs took readily enough to the life of a Cotswold country squire, making his home in the lovely old Ablington Manor and combining a life of hunting, shooting and fishing with a taste for scholarship and a lively interest in his adopted village and in the lives of its inhabitants.

The title *A Cotswold Village* is something of a misnomer. For although Ablington, intertwined with nearby Bibury, figures prominently in the book, this is really a young man's outpouring of all that the Cotswolds meant to him, with chapters on local history and characters, a range of sports, natural history, folklore, and an array of other subjects reflecting the author's love of country life in all its varied aspects.

Sadly, Gibbs died of a heart attack in 1899, the year following the publication of his book. He was only thirty-one. *A Cotswold Village,* reprinted countless times, lives on however, a fitting memorial to a remarkable Victorian country gentleman.

Recommended Reading
A Cotswold Village, J. Arthur Gibbs.

Nearby Strolls
The Poet in the Park: Alexander Pope in Cirencester Park (p100).
The Curious Traveller: H.J. Massingham at Duntisbourne Rouse (p90).

Stroud area

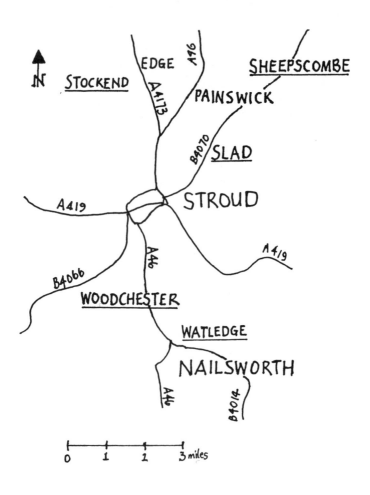

A Cotswold Year

C. Henry Warren at Stockend

Distance: 1½ miles

Location: Stockend. The hamlet lies along a no-through-road, three-quarters mile SW of Edge church and the A4173, and 3 miles NW of Stroud.

Park and Start: By the bus shelter, a short way along the unclassified road, signposted Whiteshill and Randwick, from its junction with the A4173 at Edge. (OS Landranger Sheet 162. GR 847098).

Terrain: Along minor roads, tracks and footpaths, which may be muddy after rain. A few fairly steep climbs.

Refreshments: The Edgemoor Inn, Edge (on the A4173).

Route

➤ Follow the unclassified road towards Whiteshill, passing cottages on the right, to reach a minor road, signposted Stockend. No-through-road, also on the right.

➤ Keep to the right at a fork and continue to reach a house on the left, Allanhay, just before a gate leading to Randalls Farm. This house was the home, for several years from 1932, of C. Henry Warren, and it was here that he wrote *A Cotswold Year*, which was first published in 1936.

➤ Just beyond the house, cross a stile and pass through a gate to follow the public footpath leading up to Maitlands Wood (National Trust). On crossing a stile into a lower strip of woodland, bear to the left and leave this wood over another stile.

➤ The path now skirts a garden before reaching a surfaced track. Turn left along this track and continue as far as a Cotswold Way sign on the right.

➤ Follow the Cotswold Way up into Maitlands Wood and cross the Edge – Whiteshill road to descend steps into the floor of an abandoned quarry.

➤ The route crosses the quarry floor to reach more steps leading up on to Rudge Hill Common. Extensive views now open up eastwards, with Painswick church spire dominant.

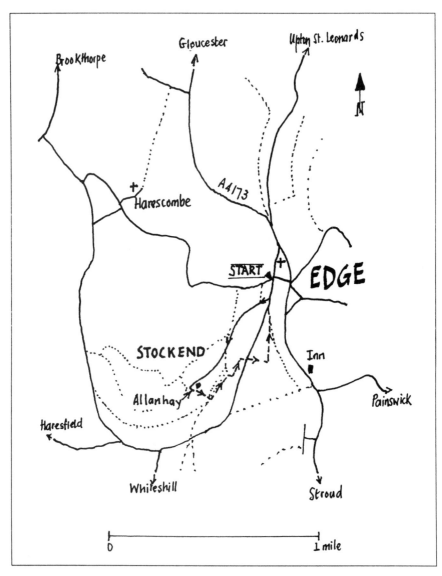

➤ Follow the Cotswold Way to the right across the Common as far as a
wide track. Turn left here, leaving the Way to make for the lower
left-hand corner of the Common. From this point, join the Edge –
Whiteshill road and turn right to pass Stockend Lane and retrace
steps to the start.

Allanhay, Stockend – former home of C. Henry Warren

Literary Connection

Although the eminent country writer C. Henry Warren (1895-1966) was born in Kent and spent the greater part of his life in Essex, during the 1930s he lived for several years in a remote corner of the Cotswolds, in a cottage called Allanhay, in the scattered hamlet of Stockend, near Edge.

This move to Gloucestershire came about through Warren's work with the BBC, which he joined in 1928 as a press officer, a job he took in an attempt to gain the financial security that his freelance writing had until then failed to provide. His radio talks, and especially a series entitled *Out And About,* not only won him a wide reputation as a fine observer of the rural scene but also led to the writing of a highly successful book, *A Cotswold Year,* based on a year's life as seen from the window of his delightfully situated cottage.

However, *A Cotswold Year* is far more than merely a cosy commentary on day-to-day life in a Cotswold hamlet. True, Woodend (Warren's name for Stockend) and its inhabitants figure prominently throughout its pages; but the author extends his range to include, among other things, keenly drawn observations on wildlife, such as the blackbird that 'will launch on the loveliest of phrases and then suddenly cease on a rasping note like the ripping of a sheet of calico' – to a plea for the teaching of local history in schools.

His comments on places visited, too, are worthy of note. Like J.B. Priestley, who took exception to Broadway's 'olde worlde' posturing, Warren thought the Worcestershire village 'a place to be looked at and admired rather than to be lived in', whereas Chipping Campden gave rise to 'the sense, everywhere, of healthy activity and inconsequent gaiety'.

It was to the lovely Essex village of Finchingfield that Henry Warren departed from Stockend and the Cotswolds. A steady flow of well-written country books followed the move, assuring him of a place among the best of 20th century rural writers.

Recommended Reading

A Cotswold Year. C. Henry Warren. Bles 1936. Reprinted Alan Sutton 1985.

The Contented Countryman. The Best of C. Henry Warren. Edited by Geoffrey Warren. Sutton 1991.

Nearby Strolls

A Lifetime in the Valley: Laurie Lee at Slad. (p114).

The Cricketing Poet: Frank Mansell at Sheepscombe. (p111).

The Cricketing Poet
Frank Mansell at Sheepscombe

Distance: 1 mile

Location: Sheepscombe. The village lies off the A46 (Cheltenham-Stroud road), 1½ miles east of Painswick, from the northern outskirts of which it is best approached.

Park and Start: Strollers patronising the Butcher's Arms Inn can make use of the car park. Otherwise, park as near as possible to the inn, from which the stroll commences. (OS Landranger Sheet 163. GR 892105).

Terrain: Starts along a minor road before climbing a steep, stony track, followed by an equally steep descent.

Refreshments: The Butcher's Arms Inn.

Route

➤ From the road junction by the Butcher's Arms Inn, walk along the no-through-road signposted Sheepscombe Far End. Pass several interesting old houses, including one on the right dated 1683, outside which is an impressive collection of horseshoes.

➤ On reaching a notice indicating the Laurie Lee Field on the left, follow the stony track (bridleway), passing old quarries and flora-rich banks. The cricket ground is reached through a gateway on the right. The views here are spectacular.

➤ Beyond the cricket ground, continue as far as a narrow winding path on the left, just before reaching woodland. Descending to the right of a well-sited seat, keep to the irregular path as it dips to follow a boundary on the right.

➤ Continue beneath trees to meet and descend along a narrow road leading to a wider road at Sheepscombe.

➤ Turn left back to the start.

Literary Connection

In sharp contrast to that of his friend and neighbour, Laurie Lee, Frank Mansell's life was confined almost exclusively to a tiny corner of the Cotswolds centred on the valleys and uplands around Sheepscombe, Bisley and Miserden.

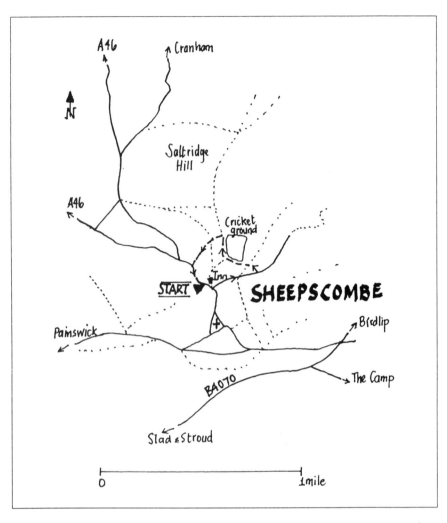

He always maintained that he could trace his ancestry back to Norman times and that he was the last of the line. What is certain is that despite having turned his back on the farming that had been his family's livelihood for generations, his love for the stone and soil of the Cotswolds never waned and gave rise to the simple and often melancholy poetry on which his reputation rests.

Mansell's other passion was village cricket. In a career spanning almost half a century, first as a boy playing for Bisley, later turning out for Miserden before finally becoming a stalwart of the Sheepscombe

Sheepscombe village

eleven, his fast bowling earned him lasting respect across the cricket fields of the Cotswolds. It is appropriate, therefore, that Sheepscombe's lovely cricket ground features on the stroll.

Frank Mansell's former home, Salt Box Cottage, still stands on the B4070 opposite the Sheepscombe turn. He is buried in Miserden churchyard, alongside his parents and not far from another local celebrity, Pat Smythe. His tombstone, beneath a cherry tree, bears the words:

'In loving memory of Frank Robert Mansell, aged 60 years, who passed away on 10 January 1979 and whose life on these hills inspired him to write verse. So about folks gone on, to where he himself has gone, may they all rest in peace'.

Recommended Reading

Cotswold Ballads. Frank Mansell. Richard Courtauld. 1974

Nearby Strolls

A Lifetime in the Valley: Laurie Lee at Slad (p114).

A Cotswold Year: C. Henry Warren at Stockend (p107).

A Lifetime in the Valley
Laurie Lee at Slad

Distance: 2 miles

Location: Slad. The village stands on the B4070, 2 miles NE of Stroud.

Park and Start: Limited parking at top of Steanbridge Lane, on left-hand side of B4070 facing Stroud, from which the stroll commences. (OS Landranger Sheet 162. GR 874075).

Terrain: Commencing with a downhill stretch of pavement walking, the route then consists chiefly of field paths, which can be muddy after rain. A few short but steep climbs.

Refreshments: Woolpack Inn.

Route

➤ From the top of Steanbridge Lane, walk along the pavement of the B4070 in the direction of Stroud. The Woolpack Inn is passed on the left. Laurie Lee's childhood home, Rosebank, lies down the slope behind the inn. Opposite is Holy Trinity church, while below, also on the right, is the former school, described so vividly in *Cider With Rosie*.

➤ Continue along the pavement and round a sharp left-hand bend. About a third of a mile beyond the bend, watch for a signposted footpath on the left opposite a postbox set in a wall.

➤ Cross a stile and descend a bank, keeping a fence on the left, to reach another stile leading to a narrow road.

➤ Turn left. The road climbs steeply and winds to a junction. Again, turn left and soon take yet another left turn, this time along a private road (public path) leading towards Upper Vatch Mill.

➤ In a short distance, leave this road over a stile on the right and follow the direction indicated by the yellow waymark, passing beneath power lines, and towards a stile alongside a gate in the hedge ahead.

➤ In the next field, aim in the direction of Furners Farm, clearly visible ahead. The path eventually dips to cross a stream by a footbridge.

➤ Beyond the bridge, the route veers to the right to reach a tree-lined lane over a stile. Turn left and climb up to Furners Farm.

> The route goes to the left to pass between the farm buildings and along a lane to enter an old orchard through a gate.
> Continue, with hedges on the right, crossing two stiles to enter a thicket. Ignore a path to the right and descend, with a fence on the left, to another stile.

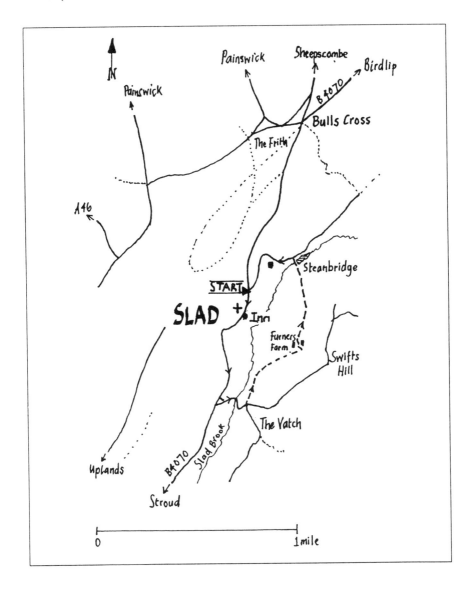

➤ The descent continues with a hedge now on the left, to reach a stile by a gate. Cross a bridge, with a lake on the right, to reach a road.

➤ This is Steanbridge. The large house on the left, on the site of a former cloth mill, featured as the squire's house in *Cider With Rosie*.

➤ Follow the narrow winding road as it climbs back to Slad and the start.

Slad

Literary Connection

No Cotswold village has a stronger or more celebrated literary connection than tiny Slad, straggling along its own intimate little valley north of Stroud. For it was here, during the First World War, that the infant Laurie Lee was set down from a carrier's cart to experience the unfurling of a life, the recapturing of which has brought delight to millions.

Cider With Rosie, first published in 1959, has sold over six million copies, has been widely used as a school textbook, and translated into many languages. It brought its author fame and fortune, yet unlike so many other famous firsts in the literary world, it in no way distanced its creator from his humble beginnings. Indeed, right up to his death, aged

82, in May 1997, Slad was Laurie Lee's home and no amount of wealth, travel or public acclaim could lure him from the village in the valley he loved.

His last achievement, and one for which all lovers of the Cotswolds should be forever grateful, was the prominent role he played a few years before his death in ensuring that the Slad Valley was saved from a vast housing development with which it had been threatened.

The short stroll in 'Laurie Lee Country' described here takes in most of the features described in *Cider With Rosie*. However, to derive the maximum amount of pleasure from exploring this corner of the Cotswolds, it is essential to read the book beforehand and if possible, to take it on the stroll and dip into it again from time to time along the way.

Recommended Reading

Cider With Rosie, Laurie Lee (Numerous hard and paperback editions).

Nearby Strolls

The Cricketing Poet: Frank Mansell at Sheepscombe (p111).

A Cotswold Year: C. Henry Warren at Stockend (p107).

The Scholar Poet's Second Home
A.E. Housman at Woodchester

Distance: 1 mile

Location: South Woodchester. The village lies off the A46, 2 miles south of Stroud. Leave the A46 at the South Woodchester and Ram Inn sign.

Park and Start: By the Ram Inn. Strollers patronising the inn can make use of the car park. Otherwise, limited roadside parking is available below the inn. (OS Landranger sheet 162. GR 838022).

Terrain: A mixture of surfaced roads and paths, with some field path walking. Warning! Although this stroll is short, the gradients are among the steepest in the book.

Refreshments: The Ram Inn.

Route

➢ From the inn, walk downhill towards the A46 to reach the war memorial. 40 metres beyond, follow the public footpath sign between two pillars (one indicating Woodchester House) and up a drive to reach a fork.

➢ For a glimpse of Woodchester House, where A.E. Housman often stayed, follow the drive a short distance to the left. The house, 18th century, solidly built with three storeys and a central pedimented door, stands masked by foliage on the right.

➢ To continue the stroll, follow the path along the perimeter of Woodchester House grounds to the right down to a metal barrier alongside gates. This leads to a surfaced path, from the top of which are wide views eastwards, dominated by the bold sweep of Minchinhampton Common.

➢ Descend the path, pass through a kissing gate and climb to the summit of the rise, from which a good view can be had of the tall spire of St Mary's church, built only a few years before Housman first stayed at Woodchester House. (The poet's parents had been married at the old church – now a ruin – at North Woodchester in 1858).

➢ The route continues along the signposted public footpath striking off sharply to the left at the top of the slope. Cross a stile and descend a grassy bank to cross a footbridge.

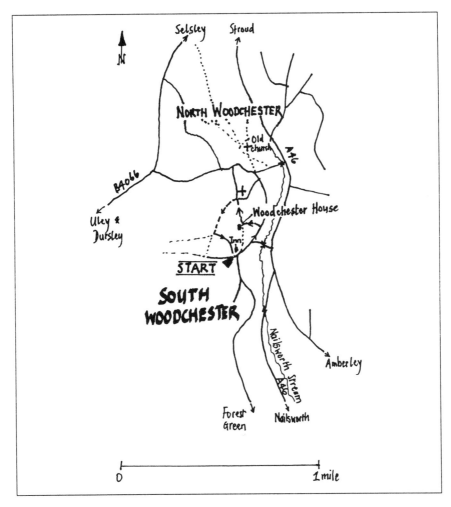

> Climb the bank to a stile, with views of Woodchester House grounds on the left, and continue on the same line to a second stile, reached up steps, to join a lane at right angles.

> This is Laggar Lane, an ancient green lane. The Ram Inn is a short distance to the left. However, strollers wishing to extend the walk for a short way, involving retracing steps, can do so by turning right along the lane, which from this point is a rough track between ancient trees and which mysteriously comes to an abrupt end in about a quarter of a mile.

Old Church and Roman villa site: As can be seen from the sketchmap, these two interesting features are within easy walking distance of the Ram Inn. The Norman church of St Mary was abandoned in 1863. The chancel arch, a doorway and a window still stand in the well-maintained churchyard, which contains several traditional Cotswold table tombs.

The 60-room Roman villa is situated to the south of the churchyard. It was excavated in the 1790s and was found to include a superb mosaic depicting Orpheus playing a lyre and surrounded by animals. It is uncovered for public inspection at rare intervals.

Literary Connection

A Worcestershire man, best known for his sequence of poems entitled *A Shropshire Lad*, Alfred Edward Housman (1859-1936) spent many of his happiest hours in Gloucestershire, staying at Woodchester House with family friends, Mr and Mrs Wise. Edward Wise was a mill owner and his wife was a close friend of Housman's mother, daughter of a former rector. After her death, when Housman was twelve, he spent an increasing amount of time at Woodchester and in so doing made lifelong friends of the three Wise children, Edith, Edward and Minnie.

After an undistinguished record at Oxford, Housman worked at the Patent Office before his reputation as a classical scholar, gained through years of private study, eventually won him professorships, first at University College, London and later at Cambridge.

Yet despite his academic attainments, Housman never lost touch with Woodchester and his friends the Wises. During the summer of 1926, he was called upon to deliver explanatory lectures on the Roman pavement re-opened in the old churchyard and it is clear from his correspondence over the years that he regarded himself almost as a 'local' in the village he had known and loved from early childhood.

Recommended Reading

The Collected Poems of A.E. Housman. Cape.

Nearby Stroll

The Tramp Poet's Last Home: W.H. Davies at Nailsworth (p121).

The Tramp-Poet's Last Home
W.H. Davies at Watledge

Distance: 1¼ miles

Location: Watledge, a hamlet off the A46, a quarter of a mile north of Nailsworth. Reached by following signs from crossroads by clock tower at Nailsworth town centre.

Park and Start: As near as possible to 'Glendower', (former home of W.H. Davies), approximately a quarter of a mile on right along Watledge road and opposite a large house (Yatesfield) with telephone box just beyond. (OS Landranger Sheet 162. GR 848004).

Terrain: Flat along road section but very steep ascents and descents of Watledge Hill. Stout footwear and sound lungs essential!

Refreshments: Choice of inns and cafes in Nailsworth.

Route

➤ From 'Glendower', walk back along the road towards Nailsworth. Immediately beyond the former Shears Inn (still bearing name) on the left, follow the public footpath sign, also on the left. The winding surfaced path climbs between houses before entering woodland (National Trust sign – Watledge Hill).

➤ Follow the main woodland path which climbs steeply. Pass a seat beneath two giant beeches on the right and keep on to reach a narrow surfaced road. Follow this to its end at a T-junction.

➤ Turn left, and in 50 metres, left again along a narrow lane. Pass houses and continue as far as a sign on the left indicating a footpath leading to Theescombe.

➤ Descend a stony track between walls as far as a stile on the right (Theescombe sign). Follow the yellow waymark down a field to enter woodland over a stile.

➤ Inside the wood, the path forks. Take the left-hand fork and descend to leave the wood over two stiles. The descent continues between walls to pass through a metal kissing gate and along a drive (18th century Dunkirk Manor on the right) to meet a road.

➤ Turn left back to the start, passing an attractive water outlet (dated 1833) on the left and a former school and teacher's house on the right.

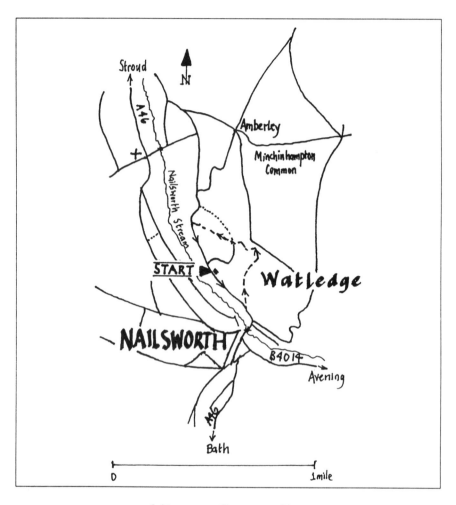

Literary Connection

'Glendower', a low, two-storey roadside cottage, was in a sad state of dereliction at the time of writing. Even so, it was still possible to decipher the words on the commemorative stone set in the wall by the door:

W.H. DAVIES, poet
Born at Newport, Mon. 1871
Died in this house 1940.

What is this life if, full of care,
We have no time to stand and stare.

'Glendower' – W.H. Davies' last house

Together with his young wife Helen, the ageing poet had moved to Glendower a mere two years earlier, after having lived in three different houses in Nailsworth since first arriving in Gloucestershire in 1931. Asked what brought him to the Cotswolds, Davies invariably replied that he wished to be near to his native Wales but not actually within its borders!

Considering the mobility problems resulting from the loss of a leg – amputated after his fall from a moving train during his youthful hobo days in Canada – and a recent stroke, it seemed strange that Davies chose to make his final home in such a steep and remote situation. Certainly Glendower's spacious garden was an attraction. We know, too, that he prepared his last collection of verse, *The Loneliest Mountain and Other Poems* here, ready for publication in 1939, and that many of his closest literary friends, including Violet Gordon Woodhouse, Osbert Sitwell and Brian Waters, visited him during the final months of an eventful life.

So although our stroll takes us over terrain that Davies, one of our greatest nature poets, would have found too steep to tackle during his 'Glendower' days, it is more than likely that he came this way while living in Nailsworth. During his time there, he wrote: 'In this little town, where I now live, there are so many circular walks that I often find it difficult to decide which to take. If the wind is strong, I usually give it my back, to be blown along. But when the morning is quiet and sunny, I go anywhere, and lean on every stile or country gate I see'.

Recommended Reading

Autobiography of a Super Tramp (1908)

Later Days (1925)

Young Emma (1980)

Collected Poems (1942)

All by W.H. Davies

Nearby Stroll

The Scholar Poet's Second Home: A.E. Housman at Woodchester. (p118).

Newent and
The Forest of Dean area

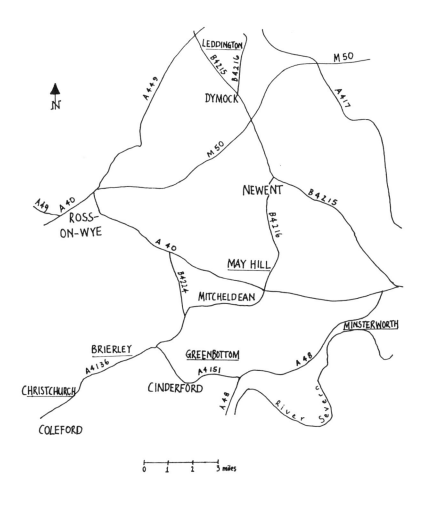

A Poet's Patch
W.W. Gibson at Leddington

Distance: 2½ miles

Location: Greenway Cross, Leddington, a crossroads on the B4216, 1½ miles north of Dymock.

Park and Start: Layby on B4216 at crossroads (OS Landranger Sheet 149. GR 703332).

Terrain: A mixture of minor roads and footpaths, which may be muddy after rain. Gentle gradients only.

Refreshments: The Beauchamp Arms, Dymock. Horseshoe Inn, Brooms Green.

Route

➤ From the crossroads, follow the unclassified road signposted Brooms Green and Bromsberrow. This quiet, gently climbing road is flanked on the left by woodland, which in spring is carpeted by daffodils and wood anemones and echoes with bird song.

➤ In rather less than half a mile, and immediately beyond a sharp left-hand bend, leave the road over a stile on the right to follow a signposted footpath. This path angles back sharply at first before veering to the left and heading off across the field which it leaves via steps into an even larger field.

➤ Like the previous field, this vast expanse is cultivated but the path at the time of writing was clearly marked as a result of spraying. Follow it to cross a footbridge and reach the B4216.

➤ Turn left and in 20 metres, right to follow a public footpath sign along the lane to Farm Mill. Beyond the timber-framed farmhouse, the path continues through a handgate to cross the River Leadon over a footbridge.

➤ Beyond the bridge, go through a field gate (yellow waymark) and cross the field along the line indicated by the arrow to reach a stile to the left of another field gate. Turn left into Pound Farm yard.

➤ Keep the buildings on the left to reach a farm track. From here a good view can be had of the farmhouse, a venerable old building, believed to be of 16th century origin, with timber framing and a hipped roof.

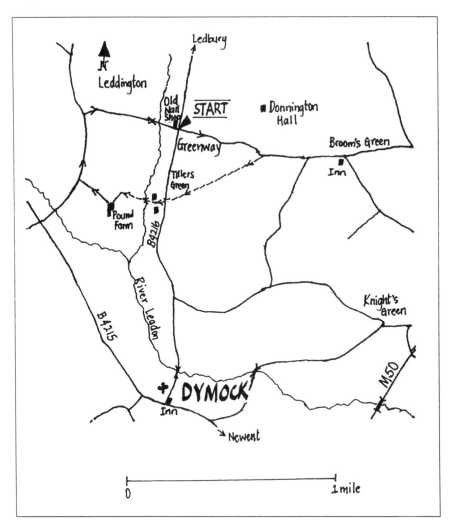

> Turn right along the track, which climbs to pass over a bridge of the dismantled railway before reaching a road.

> Turn right into the hamlet of Tillers Green and continue to reach a road junction.

> Again turn right. Cross the River Leadon once more to reach Greenway Cross by the Old Nail Shop, formerly the home of the poet W.W. Gibson.

The Old Nail Shop, Leddington

Literary Connection

Between 1913 and 1918, the Northumbrian poet Wilfrid Wilson Gibson (1878-1962) lived with his wife at The Old Nailshop, Greenway Cross, Leddington, near Dymock. Their red brick, timber-framed cottage, complete with thatched roof, was so called through having been for many years previously the home of a family named Saddler who were nail-makers.

Gibson had been drawn to Gloucestershire through his friendship with a fellow poet, Lascelles Abercrombie, who lived at Ryton, near Dymock, and the two were responsible for establishing the so-called 'Muse Colony', which was to include Rupert Brooke, John Drinkwater, Edward Thomas and Robert Frost, and which flourished briefly during 1914.

Although virtually unheard of today, Gibson was a highly successful poet between the wars and was especially known for his down-to-earth verse featuring the lives of the common people, then something of a novelty in the world of poetry. Such poems as *Flannan Isle* and *The Ice Cart* appeared regularly in anthologies and Gibson's readings of his work were in great demand both in this country and the United States.

Gibson's brief tenancy of The Old Nailshop was commemorated by two richly atmospheric poems based on the house itself. In *The Old Nailshop*, he evokes the time long before when his cottage had echoed

> *"With hammers heating red-hot wire*
> *On tinkling anvils by the fire*
> *To ten-a-penny nails"*

While in *The Golden Room*, written more than a decade after the occasion, he recalls a still July evening in 1914 when the poets and their wives had gathered in his cottage "for talk and laughter on a summer night", and laments that two of their number, Rupert Brooke and Edward Thomas, were to die within three years of that happy event.

Although Abercrombie's house at Ryton has long since disappeared, two other houses associated with the Dymock poets have survived. Little Iddens, home of the American poet, Robert Frost, and Oldfields, where Edward Thomas lived during August 1914, can still be seen at Leddington, a short distance to the north of the Old Nailshop.

In addition, two waymarked 'Poets' Paths' can be followed in the area (see tourist information centres for details).

Recommended Reading

Collected Poems. W.W. Gibson (Macmillan 1926).

The Golden Room. W.W. Gibson (Macmillan 1938).

For detailed accounts of the 'Muse Colony', see *The Muse Colony*. Keith Clark. (Redcliffe 1992).

The Dymock Poets. Sean Street. (Seren. 1994).

Once they lived in Gloucestershire, Linda Hart. (Green Branch 1995).

Nearby Stroll

Man of Many Parts: John Haines on May Hill (p130).

Man of Many Parts
John Haines on May Hill

Distance: 1¼ miles

Location: May Hill, one of Gloucestershire's most prominent landmarks, lies one mile north of the A40 at Dursley Cross, between Newent and Mitcheldean.

Park and Start: Layby opposite May Hill sign along Yartleton Lane, reached from A40 at Dursley Cross (see sketch map). (OS Landranger Sheet 162, GR691211).

Terrain: Along grassy paths throughout, which may be muddy after rain. A short, steep climb followed by a gentler descent.

Refreshments: The Glasshouse Inn, Glasshouse. Yew Tree Inn, Clifford's Mesne.

Route

➤ Follow the direction indicated by the May Hill signpost. The footpath climbs to the left of a chalet-type house.

➤ Cross a stile and climb steps through woodland to emerge on the lower slopes of the hill through a gate.

➤ A short, if steep climb leads to the conifer-topped summit, on which stands a triangulation pillar at 296 metres (969 feet) above sea level and a small monument commemorating jubilees of Queen Victoria and Queen Elizabeth II.

➤ As May Hill is the property of the National Trust, there are no access restrictions and an enjoyable ramble can be taken around the summit and lower slopes, offering superb views in all directions on a clear day.

➤ To resume the stroll, follow the wide grassy path descending to the left of the triangulation pillar. On approaching within 60 metres of a gate ahead, turn sharp right at a marker post to reach a stile leading into woodland.

➤ Follow the delightful gently descending woodland footpath for about half a mile to rejoin the outward route by the house passed at the start of the stroll.

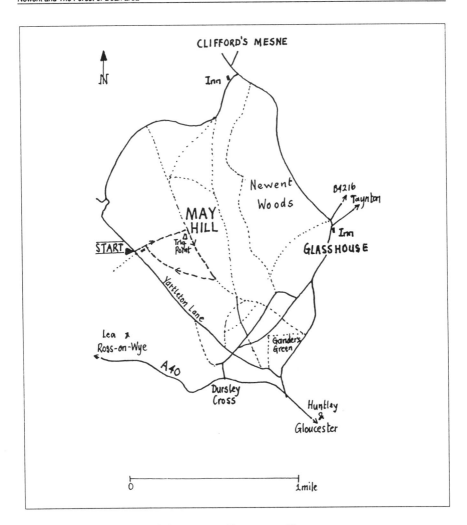

Literary Connection

Once known as Yartleton Hill, May Hill gets its name from two ancient May Day customs. One of these related to the rights held by the commoners of the nearby parishes, representatives of whom met on the hill on May Day morning to resolve any disputes concerning the common. In the other, and more colourful custom, young local people enacted a symbolic battle on the hill between winter and summer, after which the victorious summer party carried home budding branches and spring flowers as tokens of their season's triumph.

Sheep on May Hill

The clump of conifers crowning the summit of the hill was planted in 1887 to commemorate Queen Victoria's Golden Jubilee. The trees replaced the storm-battered specimens described by John Masefield, as seen from his childhood home at Ledbury, and which he imagined as a giant ploughman "driving his team against the sky".

In 1914, as the First World War loomed, two of the so-called Dymock poets, the American Robert Frost and his new-found friend Edward Thomas, delighted in their discovery of May Hill. Both owed this pleasure to a mutual friend, John Haines. Haines, a solicitor by profession, lived at Hucclecote near Gloucester, and shared a love of poetry and the countryside with a fellow solicitor, Will Harvey (see *A Gloucestershire Lad* F.W. Harvey at Minsterworth. p143).

He was also a highly competent and enthusiastic botanist, specialising in the plants of the Newent and Forest of Dean areas and at the suggestion of another locally-based poet, Lascelles Abercrombie, he invited Frost, himself a keen plant hunter, to accompany him on a botanising expedition to May Hill, which the poet recalled fondly later, and which led to a lifelong friendship.

Edward Thomas, too, shared a lasting love of wild flowers and it followed that the three men rejoiced in their days spent wandering on and around May Hill. It was after one of Thomas's cycling trips to the hill with Haines that his friend wrote: "Whilst I botanised on the hill slopes, he sat on the hill dreaming over the distant hills of Wales, and composing the beautiful poem *Words*, which he brought down completed for us at breakfast next morning."

Although Robert Frost returned to America in 1915, his friendship with John Haines resulted in two more visits to Gloucestershire. On the first of these, in 1928, the two friends once again climbed May Hill. Their thoughts and conversation turned inevitably to Edward Thomas, prompting Frost to write: "The wraith of that dead friend was ever before us."

Recommended Reading

The Muse Colony. Keith Clark. Redcliffe. 1992.

The Dymock Poets. Sean Street. Seren, 1994.

Once they lived in Gloucestershire. Linda Hart. Green Branch, 1995.

Nearby Strolls

A Poet's Patch: W.H.Gibson at Leddington (p126).

A Fool in the Forest: Leonard Clark at Green Bottom (p137).

The Child in The Forest
Winifred Foley at Brierley

Distance: 2¼ miles

Location: Brierley. The village stands on the A4136, one mile east of its junction with the B4234 and approximately midway between Mitcheldean and Coleford.

Park and start: As near as possible to the Swan Inn, from which the stroll begins. (OS Landranger Sheet 162. GR 626152).

Terrain: Chiefly along forest paths, though with a few stretches of roadside verge walking. Gentle gradients only.

Refreshments: Swan Inn, Brierley.

Route

➤ Facing the inn, turn right (i.e. towards Mitcheldean) and walk the few yards to reach open woodland on the left beyond the last house. A track, somewhat indistinct to begin with, climbs through the trees with houses on the left. Eventually this track joins a surfaced access road. The modernised and extended white house immediately ahead, named Kate's Cottage, was the childhood home of Winifred Foley.

➤ Soon the access road swings to the left to join the Brierley – Ruardean road. Turn right along the ample verge and continue for almost three-quarters of a mile, passing the tree-clad spoilheap of a long-abandoned colliery on the left before reaching a road, also on the left, signposted Newham Bottom.

➤ Follow this road, passing Ruardean Woodside school, attended by the young Winifred, on the right. Ignore a signposted footpath climbing on the right and continue as far as a roughly-surfaced lane descending sharply to the left opposite a cottage.

➤ Beyond another cottage, the route continues as a narrow path, which descends, with trees on the left, to cross a stream over a tiny concrete bridge. From this bridge, climb the bank ahead for about 30 metres to reach a well-used cross path. Turn left along this delightful woodland path, which follows the stream just crossed down its tiny valley for about half a mile to reach a wide surfaced track.

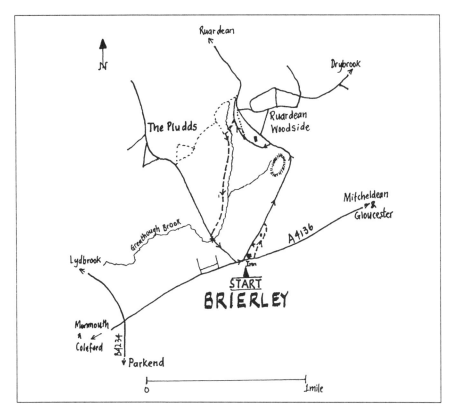

> Turn right along this track and follow it the short distance to reach the Brierley – Pludds road via a traffic barrier. Turn left along the verge back to the Swan Inn and the start.

Literary Connection

It was in the early 1970s that a middle-aged Gloucestershire woman sent a collection of her childhood memories to the BBC. By happy chance, these scribbles (the author's own description) caught the eye of a sympathetic producer and *A Child In The Forest* was born.

Apart from a few magazine articles and a contribution included in a book on working-class lives submitted to a professor of social history in response to a newspaper advertisement, Winifred Foley had never considered herself to be a writer.

The daughter of a Forest of Dean miner who had lost his life underground, Winifred had been born and bred at the little village of Brierley, deep in the Forest. Leaving school at 14, she had 'gone into service', first locally, then in London, where she met her future husband. Her native Forest had drawn her back however, and she and her husband had quietly raised their family in modest circumstances not far from her childhood home.

Now, all this was to change. In 1973, Winifred's early memories were serialised on Woman's Hour. The BBC followed this up with *A Child In The Forest* in book form and some time later an episode from the book was successfully adapted for television under the title *Abide With Me*.

Other books followed: each one revealing some new aspect of the hard yet basically happy lives of Forest people in the inter-war years. Winifred Foley's books have been called earthy, unsentimental and stark. So they are. Yet there is warmth, and humour too, in plenty, and to those who know and love the Forest of Dean and its people, Winifred Foley stands alongside Flora Thompson as a gifted and faithful chronicler of the corner of England in which she was raised.

Recommended Reading

A Child In The Forest
No Pipe Dreams for Father
Back to the Forest
In and Out of the Forest
(All by Winifred Foley).

Nearby Strolls

The Playwright in his Place: Dennis Potter at Christchurch (p140).
A Fool in The Forest: Leonard Clark at Green Bottom (p137).

A Fool in The Forest
Leonard Clark at Green Bottom

Distance: 1¾ miles

Location: Green Bottom. The hamlet lies 1½ miles north of the A4151 at Littledean.

Park and Start: By the Beulah Chapel (O.S. Landranger Sheet 162. GR673153).

Terrain: A mixture of minor roads and forest tracks and paths, which can be muddy after rain. Gentle gradients.

Refreshments: Choice of inns in Littledean

Route

➤ From the chapel, follow the road south (i.e. uphill) out of the hamlet. On reaching a junction, continue straight on and over the brow.

➤ Turn left along the second track on the left, opposite Pike House Cottage. On reaching a bungalow, turn left down a track.

➤ Pass another bungalow and continue down a wide grassy path to meet a track alongside woodland (Chestnuts Inclosure).

➤ Turn left and follow the track the short distance to reach another track, with a house standing in spacious grounds on the right and a forest barrier alongside. (Note: – Those wishing to extend the stroll can enjoy a pleasant detour into the Inclosure by turning right past the barrier).

➤ To return to Green Bottom, cross straight over the track and follow the narrow woodland path. Ignore a side path to the right. The path soon dips to reach a wider path, with the road junction passed earlier visible below

➤ Turn left to reach the junction. To pass Tibbs Cross Farm and enter Green Bottom from the northern approach, turn right. The turn to Green Bottom is on the left beyond Tibbs Cross.

Literary Connection

No mean poet himself, Leonard Clark was best known for his popular anthologies of poetry for children. Between 1936 and 1970, he served as an inspector of schools (HMI) working in Devon, Yorkshire and London

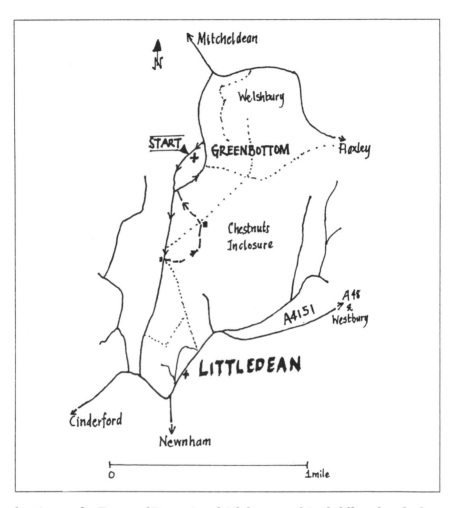

but it was the Forest of Dean , in which he spent his childhood and adolescence, that he loved most, and about which he wrote with warmth many years later in his autobiographical *Green Wood* and *A Fool in the Forest*.

Clark's boyhood home was at Cinderford and his teaching career commenced as a 17 year old student at the senior school there at a salary of £2.7s.6d per month. It was at about this time that he commenced his solitary explorations of the Forest, beginning with Abbots Wood, south of Cinderford, a memorable description of which appears in *Green Wood*.

Cottages at Green Bottom

However, it was to the area around Chestnuts Wood, away to the east of Cinderford, that Leonard Clark devoted the greater part of his descriptive writing on the Forest. In *The Ruined Forest*, the opening chapter of *A Fool In The Forest*, he recalls that "the map of the Chestnuts Wood, with Greenway Farm, Tibbs Cross, Badcocks Barley and Morpeth Point was indelibly written on my heart's memory".

To Clark's dismay, the Chestnuts Wood he loved so much and which had been planted in 1812, was clear-felled during the Second World War. Much has been replanted since however, and in this quiet corner of his beloved Forest we can experience a good deal of the delight that Leonard Clark discovered there 70 or more years ago.

Recommended Reading

Green Wood. Leonard Clark. Parrish 1962. *A Fool in the Forest.* Leonard Clark. Dobson 1965.

Nearby Strolls

The Child in The Forest: Winifred Foley at Brierley (p134).

The Playwright in his Place: Dennis Potter at Berry Hill (p140).

The Playwright in his Place
Dennis Potter at Christchurch

Distance: 2¾ miles

Location: Braceland. This is a campsite and adventure centre, situated to the west of the B4432 at Christchurch, 1 mile NW of its junction with the A4136, north of Coleford. Follow the Camp Site signpost along Bracelands Drive.

Park and Start: Park in the small woodland clearing on the right, opposite the campsite office. The stroll starts from here. (OS Landranger Sheet 162. GR 568129).

Terrain: Forest tracks and paths virtually throughout, which may be muddy after rain. Gradients are gentle. (Watch also for tree-felling warning notices).

Refreshments: Choice of inns at Berry Hill or Coleford.

Route

➤ Follow the Braceland signpost (rather than walk along the surfaced road, use the path on the bank alongside). Pass the road to the Adventure Centre on the right.

➤ On reaching the campsite entrance on the right (telephone point), keep straight on along a forest track, which winds its way between the trees. Ignore all side tracks and paths. Glimpses of the campsite can be had on the right at first. The hill on the left is called Coalpit Hill, a reminder of its industrial past.

➤ Eventually the route has woodland on either side. One particularly large tree on the left of the track is labelled Braceland Larch, a magnificent specimen.

➤ Later, extensive views across the forest open out away to the left. The track now swings to the right and climbs past the entrance to the Adventure Centre to reach the outward route by a house.

➤ Turn left and retrace steps to the start.

Literary Connection

The controversial television playwright Dennis Potter was born at Berry Hill, near Coleford, in 1935, the son of a Forest miner. Determined to become a writer, he joined the BBC after leaving Oxford, where he had ed-

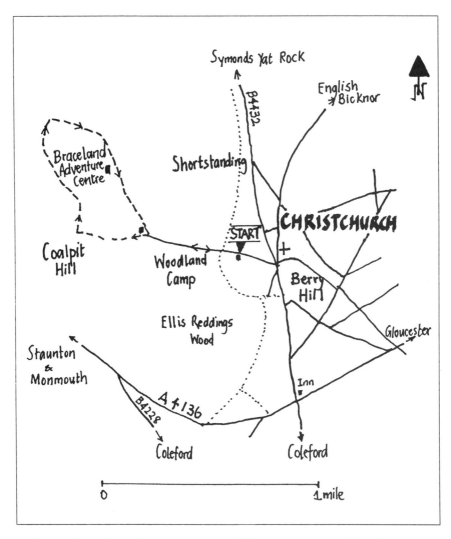

ited Isis, the University magazine, and also experimented with various literary forms before finding his ideal medium in television drama.

Several of Potter's early plays, such as *The Beast with two Backs* and *Blue Remembered Hills*, were set in his beloved Forest and he continued to draw freely on his Dean upbringing in much of his later work.

In his book, *The Changing Forest. Life in the Forest of Dean Today*, written when he was 26, Dennis Potter gives an intimate and perceptive account of the region in which he was born and bred and of the changes

The church at Christchurch

that were transforming it at that time. The book focuses especially on the closure of the local deep-mine collieries and on the effect this had on the mining communities he knew so well.

Determined to see for himself what conditions in the Forest mines were like, Potter persuaded a miner in one of the small private pits to allow him to pay a visit underground. This mine – merely two tunnels driven into a bank – was situated at Braceland, half a mile or so from Berry Hill, in the heart of the Forest. It has long since ceased working, as have all the other local mines, although telltale signs of mining activity – spoil heaps and fenced-off shafts – can still be found among the trees.

Dennis Potter never lost his affinity with his native Forest, settling eventually at nearby Ross-on-Wye. He died in 1994.

Recommended Reading

The Changing Forest. Life in the Forest of Dean Today. Dennis Potter. Secker and Warburg. 1962. (Reprinted by Minerva, 1996).

Nearby Strolls

The Child in the Forest: Winifred Foley at Brierley (p134).

A Fool in the Forest: Leonard Clark at Green Bottom (p137).

A Gloucestershire Lad
F.W. Harvey at Minsterworth

Distance: 3 miles

Location: Minsterworth lies off the A48, 4 miles west of Gloucester.

Park and Start: The church car park, opposite the church on Church Lane (signposted from A48) at the western extremity of the village. (O.S. Landranger Sheet 162. GR 774170).

Terrain: The outward route is along footpaths (numerous stiles) while the return is along quiet lanes. Level throughout.

Refreshments: The Apple Tree Inn.(on A48, halfway along route).

Route

➤ From the church car park, turn right along the road to reach a lane on the left immediately beyond the churchyard. This leads to a footpath along the flood bank of the River Severn.

➤ Turn left along this path (noticing the yellow Gloucestershire Way marks) and follow it, crossing over stiles, and ignoring side paths to the left.

➤ In about a mile, and about 40 metres before reaching a stile with power lines ahead, turn along another path curving inland towards a sluice. Follow this path round to the left to cross a stile.

➤ The route now keeps a ditch and hedge on the right, crosses an improvised stile and continues to reach another stile by a house, the drive of which leads to a road.

➤ Cross straight over and keep a boundary on the left to reach a road junction. Cross straight over to another stile on the right.

➤ Continue, crossing two more stiles. In the last field, pass a hedge corner on the left to reach a stile leading to a lay-by alongside the A48.

➤ Turn left. A good view can now be had of Redlands, the handsome Georgian farmhouse where Will Harvey spent his boyhood, standing opposite across the busy road.

➤ To complete the stroll, turn left along Watery Lane, immediately before the Apple Tree Inn. At the road junction passed earlier, turn left. The lane soon swings sharply to the right and meanders back, via Calcutt's Green, to the church and the start.

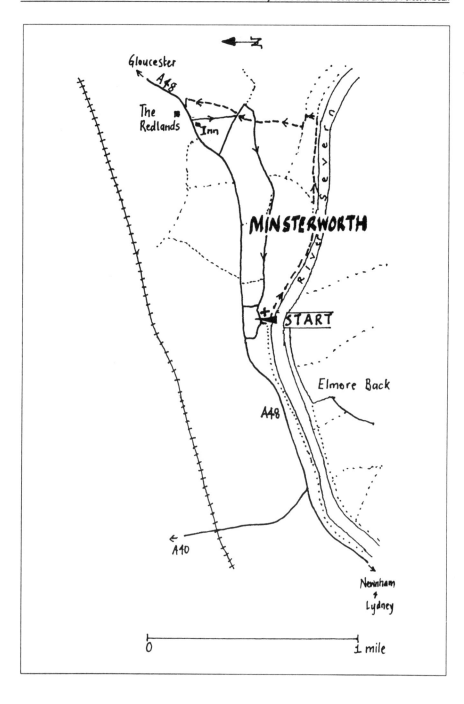

Literary Connection

Frederick William ('Will') Harvey (1888-1957) was born at Murrell's End, Hartpury, north of Gloucester, the eldest child of a prosperous horse breeder and dealer. Two years later, the family moved to Redlands, a Georgian farmhouse at Minsterworth and it was here that Will Harvey enjoyed a happy childhood and youth. And although he spent his later years at Yorkley, in the Forest of Dean, it was in Minsterworth churchyard that he was buried, in the family plot beneath an ancient yew tree.

A lawyer by profession, Harvey was at heart a true countryman and his yearning for the outdoor life found expression in poetry. Like his close friend, Ivor Gurney, his love of his native county was deep and sustaining, and helped him in no small way to survive the ordeal of captivity in a German prison camp after having been awarded the DCM for bravery in battle. His *In Flanders* dates from this period:

'I'm homesick for my hills again -
My hills again!
To see above the Severn plain
Unscabbarded against the sky
The blue high blade of Cotswold lie.'

Ironically, it is for a light-hearted poem, *Ducks*, that Will Harvey is best known, outside Gloucestershire at least. Within the county, a long-overdue revival of interest in his work, prompted by Anthony Boden's biography, has led to Harvey's poems being reprinted. Among these, appropriately enough, is *My Village*, a tribute to the poet's beloved place, its orchards, its birds, its tidal river, and above all, its people

'I love old Minsterworth. I love the men
The fishers and the cider-makers and
All who laugh and labour on that land
With humour and long patience loved of God.'

Recommended Reading

F.W Harvey. Collected Poems 1912-1957 (McLean 1983)

A Gloucestershire Lad at Home and Abroad (McLean 1988)

The Laureate of Gloucestershire. Frances Townsend (Redcliffe Press 1988).

F.W. Harvey. Soldier, Poet. Anthony Boden (Sutton Publishing 1988).

Nearby Stroll

A Fool in the Forest: Leonard Clark at Green Bottom (p137).

Minsterworth church

Bibliography

These entries are supplementary to the recommended reading on individual strolls

A Literary Tour of Gloucestershire and Bristol. David Carroll. Sutton 1994.

A Gloucestershire Gallery. Nigel Scotland (Ed) Cheltenham Tourism. 1993.

Gloucestershire Worthies. Aylwin Sampson. Westcountry Books. 1996.

Poets' England – 2. Gloucestershire. Guy Stapleton (Comp). Brentham Press. 1977.

Forest and Vale and High Blue Hill. Johnny Coppin (selected by). Windrush Press.1991.

Cotswold Follies and Fancies. Margaret Caine and Alan Gorton. S.B. Publications. 1998.

Discovering Cotswold Villages. Gordon Ottewell. Sigma Press. 1997.

Tourist Information Centres

Broadway: 1, Cotswold Court – (01386) 852937

Burford: The Brewery, Sheep Street – (01993) 823558

Cheltenham: 77 The Promenade – (01242) 522878

Chipping Campden: Unit 2, Rosary Cottage, High Street – (01386) 841206

Chipping Norton: The Guildhall, Goddards Lane – (01608) 644379

Cirencester: Corn Hall, Market Place – (01285) 654180

Coleford: High Street – (01594) 812388

Gloucester: 28 Southgate Street – (01452) 421188

*Keynes Country Park: Shorncote, Cirencester – (01285) 861459

Ledbury: 3 The Homend – 01531 636147

Moreton-in-Marsh: District Council Offices, High Street – (01608) 650881

Nailsworth: 1 Fountain Street – (01453) 832532

Newent: 7 Church Street – (01531) 822468

*Northleach: Cotswold Heritage Centre – (01451) 860715

*Painswick: The Library, Stroud Road – (01452) 813552

Stow-on-the-Wold: Hollis House, The Square – (01451) 831082

Stroud: Subscription Rooms, George Street – (01453) 765768

Tetbury: 33 Church Street – (01666) 503552

Tewkesbury: 64 Barton Street – (01684) 295027

*Winchcombe: Town Hall, High Street – (01242) 602925

Witney: 51a Market Square – (01993) 775802

Woodstock: Oxfordshire Museum, Fletcher's House, Park Street – (01993) 813276

Wotton-under-Edge: Heritage Centre, The Chipping – (01453) 521541

*Denotes limited opening only

Index

A

Abercrombie, Lascelles 128, 132
Ablington 103 - 105
Adlestrop 40 - 42
Allahakbarries, The 16
Anderson, Mary 10, 16
Archers, The 75
Asquith, Lady Cynthia 15
Asthall 69
Atkyns, Sir Robert 99
Austen, Jane 40 - 41

B

Baker, Sir Benjamin 52
Barnsley brothers 96, 99
Barrie, J.M. 11, 13
Bathurst, Allen, Lord 100 - 101
Beerbohm, Max 93 - 94
Betjeman, John 32, 34
Braceland 140, 142
Bredon Hill 4, 23, 58
Brierley 134 - 135
Broadway 8, 10 - 11, 16, 110
Brooke, Rupert 128 - 129

C

Christchurch 136, 140
Cirencester Park 90, 95, 100 - 102, 105
Clairemont, Charles 85
Clark, Leonard 137
Cobbett, William 65
Cockerell, Samuel Pepys 34
Coln St Aldwyns 82
Coln, River 66 - 67
Comper, Ninian 13
Crickley Hill 58
Cripps, Sir Stafford 76
Cutsdean 17, 19

D

Davies, W.H. 94, 120 - 122
Daylesford 43
Derrick, Freda 54
Doyle, Sir Arthur Conan 16
Drinkwater, John 93
Ducklington 73
Dugdale family 34
Dugdale, Ethel 34

Dunt, River 90
Duntisbourne Rouse 90
Duntisbourne, Middle 90

E

Eastleaches 80
Elgar, Sir Edward 11
Evenlode, River 33, 40, 44, 46

F

Far Oakridge 93 - 94
Filkins 76
Fisher, Alexander 15
Foley, Winifred 134
Ford 16
Fowler, William Warde 46
Frome, River 94, 96
Frost, Robert 128 - 129, 132
Froude, Hurrell 82

G

Gibbs, J. Arther 103
Gibson, W.W. 126
Gill, Eric 15
Gimson, Ernest 88, 96, 98
Gissing, Algernon 6
Godwin, Mary 85
Green Bottom 137
Grisewood, Freddy 43
Gurney, Ivor 58

H

Haines, John 130
Harris, Mollie 73
Harvey, F.W. 132
Hastings, Warren 43, 45
Herbert, A.P. 16
Housman, A.E. 11, 118

I

Idbury 50

J

Jack, George 88
Jewson, Norman 93, 96
Jones, Jessie 52

K

Keble College 82

Keble, John 79
Kelmscott 86
Kemerton 3
Kingham 46
Knight, Sid 11

L

Leach, River 79, 83
Lechlade 83
Leckhampton Hill 54
Leddington 126
Lee, Laurie 111, 114
Leigh, James Henry 41
Leigh, Rev. Thomas 40 - 41
Lower Slaughter 36

M

MacArthur, Wilson 17
Macarthur-Onslow, Annette 62
Mansell, Frank 111
'Mansfield Park' 42
Masefield, John 132
Mason, A.E.W. 16
Massingham, H.J. 90
May Hill 58, 130
Minsterworth 143
Mitford, Jessica & Nancy 69
Moore, John 3
Morris, William 86
'Muse Colony' 128

O

Oddington 43
Owlpen Manor 99

P

Peacock, Thomas Love 85
Pinswell (Upper Coberley) 62
Pope, Alexander 100
Potter, Dennis 140
Prescott 23
Priestley, J.B. 110

R

Repton, Humphry 42
Robertson Scott, J.W. 50
Rolt, L.T.C. 23
Rossetti, Dante Gabriel 88
Rothenstein, Sir William 93 - 94

S

Saintbury 6, 9
Sapperton 96
Severn, River 143

Seymour, Aubrey 28
Sezincote (Longborough) 32
Sheepscombe 111
Shelley, Percy 83
Sitwell, Osbert 123
Slad 114
Smith, William 6, 8
Smythe, Pat 113
Southrop 79
Stanley Pontlarge 5
Stanway 13
Stockend (Edge) 107
Stoneleigh Abbey 42
Strong, Timothy 14
Swinbrook 69, 71
Swinford, George 76

T

Taddington 17
Temple Guiting 21
Thames Path 84
Thames, River 83, 84
Thames-Severn Canal 96
Thomas, Edward 40, 132

U

Upper Ditchford 28
Upper Slaughter 36

W

Walpole, Hugh 11
Warren, C. Henry 107
Waters, Brian 123
Watledge (Nailsworth) 121
Webb, Philip 88
Wells, H.G. 16
Wemyss, Earl 15
Westerling, Margaret 16
Widford 69
Wilberforce, Robert 82
Willersey 6
Williams, Isaac 82
Withington 65
Witts, Francis 36
Woodchester 118
Woodhouse, Lady Violet Gordon 123

Y

Yorkley 145
Young, Charles Baring 45
Young, Francis Brett 11

Also of Interest:

DISCOVERING COTSWOLD VILLAGES

Gordon Ottewell

"Here, in one compact book, is a practical guide for all those who wish to visit - and explore - the most attractive villages in the Cotswolds. Read about the villages, find out about their history, then enjoy one of 50 pleasant walks to uncover the intriguing past of these... settlements". WORCESTER EVENING NEWS. £6.95

DISCOVERY WALKS IN THE COTSWOLDS

Julie Meech

Concentrating on the Cotswold heartland, this book of 20 walks avoids the obvious routes in favour of quieter footpaths - even the keenest local walker will find something new to discover. The walks give equal prominence to the natural landscape and the built environment, reflecting the harmony between the two. The rambler can thus expect to explore beautiful villages and historic market towns as well as the open wold. Nor is this book just for the motorist - every walk is easily accessible by public transport. £6.95

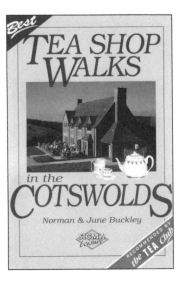

BEST TEA SHOP WALKS IN THE COTSWOLDS

Norman and June Buckley

No other area in Britain has as many tea shops as the Cotswolds. This new book of 26 walks takes the reader the length and breadth of the area, visiting the popular towns and tiny villages. The walks average 5-6 miles and each features a tea shop that welcomes walkers. £6.95

BEST PUB WALKS IN
THE COTSWOLDS
Laurence Main

The Cotswolds provide many excellent walking opportunities, plus the chance to discover its unique and characterful pubs. Let Laurence show you around! £6.95

A YEAR OF WALKS:
THE COTSWOLDS
Roy Woodcock

These 12 circular walks, one for each month of the year, visit a range of exceptional locations in the Cotswolds. You have the option of a full or half-day walk to each spot, whilst the month-by-month approach encourages you to walk in harmony with the changing seasons - dispelling the false perception of walking as an activity suitable only for summer. Especially enlightening for locals, the book will give new experience and insight to a popular region. £6.95

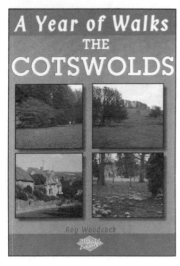

BEST TEA SHOP WALKS IN
OXFORDSHIRE
Julie Meech

The Cotswolds, the Chilterns, the Thames Valley and even a small share of the Wessex Downs - all these are to be found in Oxfordshire, yet the county's great potential for walkers is often not fully appreciated. The 25 walks in this new guide explore all the different facets of this varied county, and all include the additional pleasure of a stop for afternoon tea. Every walk is easily accessible by public transport, and many are within easy reach of London - the ideal excuse to escape from the city for a few hours! £6.95

All of our books are available through your local bookseller.
In case of difficulty, or for a free catalogue, please contact:

SIGMA LEISURE, 1 SOUTH OAK LANE, WILMSLOW, CHESHIRE SK9 6AR.
Phone: 01625-531035; Fax: 01625-536800.
E-mail: info@sigmapress.co.uk.   Web site: http//www.sigmapress.co.uk
VISA and MASTERCARD welcome.